# CONTENTS

There's a show on TV where four wildly excited guests, egged on by a wildly excited audience, bid against each other for fabulous prizes. While the rules of this game are too complicated for idiots like us to understand, the general idea is that the guest who bids closest to the actual retail price of the gift, without going over it, gets

# THE NIGHT THE PRICE IS ALL RIGHT

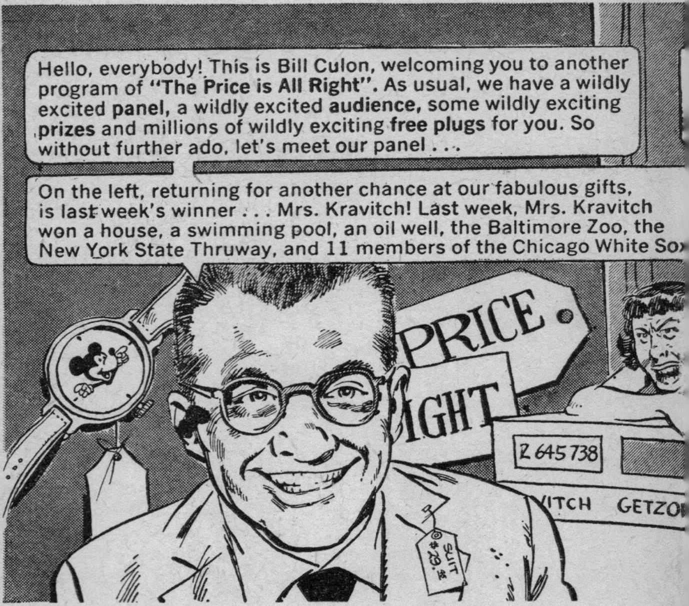
Hello, everybody! This is Bill Culon, welcoming you to another program of "The Price is All Right". As usual, we have a wildly excited panel, a wildly excited audience, some wildly exciting prizes and millions of wildly exciting free plugs for you. So without further ado, let's meet our panel . . .
On the left, returning for another chance at our fabulous gifts, is last week's winner . . . Mrs. Kravitch! Last week, Mrs. Kravitch won a house, a swimming pool, an oil well, the Baltimore Zoo, the New York State Thruway, and 11 members of the Chicago White Sox
PRICE
IGHT
2 645 738
VITCH
GETZO
SUIT $29.98

# William M. Gaines's
# GREASY
# MAD
## STUFF

## ALBERT B. FELDSTEIN, Editor

*A SIGNET BOOK*

Published by THE NEW AMERICAN LIBRARY

*Published as a SIGNET BOOK*
*by arrangement with E. C. Publications, Inc.,*
*who have authorized this softcover edition.*

FIRST PRINTING, OCTOBER, 1963

SIGNET TRADEMARK REG. U.S. PAT. OFF. AND FOREIGN COUNTRIES
REGISTERED TRADEMARK—MARCA REGISTRADA
HECHO EN CHICAGO, U.S.A.

*SIGNET BOOKS are published by*
*The New American Library of World Literature, Inc.*
*501 Madison Avenue, New York, New York 10022*

PRINTED IN THE UNITED STATES OF AMERICA

# YOU HAVE JUST DISCOVERED THE CURE FOR

## ADVERTISING'S BALD-FACED LIES!
## HOLLYWOOD'S SLICK PRODUCTIONS!
## TELEVISION'S DRY VAST WASTELAND!

✳ ✳ ✳ ✳ ✳

### Mainly because you are about to use that

# GREASY
# MAD
# STUFF

✳ ✳ ✳ ✳ ✳

Try our "30-Day Treatment" and see for yourself . . .
Rub only:

**HILARIOUS SATIRE**
**RIDICULOUS PARODY**
**LUDICROUS COMEDY**
and **ZANY ARTWORK**

into your head for 30 days!

✳ ✳ ✳ ✳ ✳

## YOUR APPEARANCE WILL CHANGE IMMEDIATELY!
Your eyes will stare vacantly!
Your tongue will droop stupidly!
Your ears will wiggle incessantly!
And your hair will <u>remain the same!</u>

## —BUT WITH ALL THOSE OTHER CHANGES, NO ONE WILL NOTICE!

## More of William M. Gaines's
## MAD Humor from SIGNET

## And by MAD'S Maddest Artist,
## Don Martin

TO OUR READERS: If your dealer does not have the SIGNET and MENTOR books you want, you may order them by mail enclosing the list price plus 5¢ a copy to cover mailing. If you would like our free catalog, please request it by postcard. The New American Library of World Literature, Inc., P.O. Box 2310, Grand Central Station, New York, New York, 10017.

to keep it. The most wonderful part of this game, aside from the fabulous items and free plugs involved, is the way the panel and the audience sustain their fever-pitch of excitement throughout the show. Which is why we feel that it's only a matter of time before a big catastrophe occurs. Mainly, on . . .

# HAS AN UNEXCITED GUEST

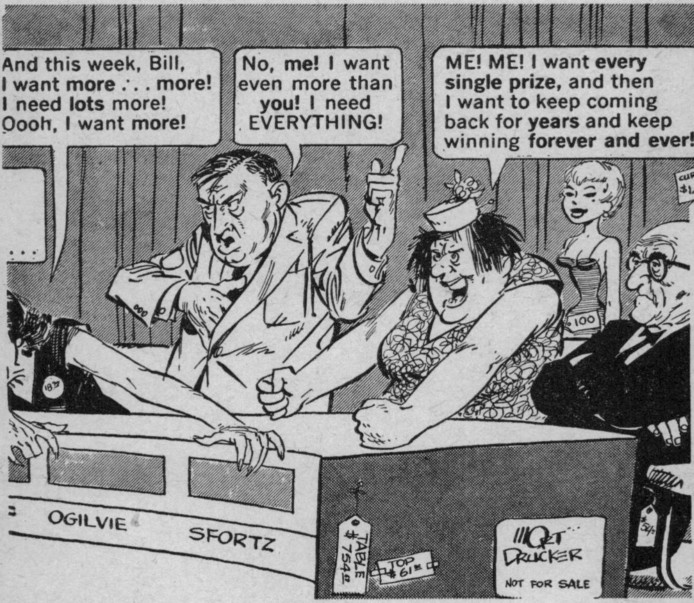

And this week, Bill, I want more . . . more! I need lots more! Oooh, I want more!
No, me! I want even more than you! I need EVERYTHING!
ME! ME! I want every single prize, and then I want to keep coming back for years and keep winning forever and ever!
OGILVIE
SFORTZ
TABLE $754.⁰⁰
TOP $61.⁰⁰
MORT DRUCKER
NOT FOR SALE

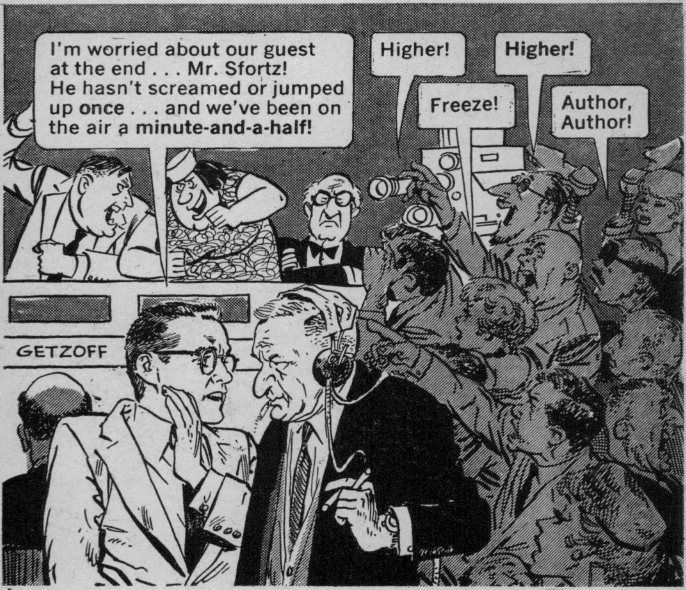
I'm worried about our guest at the end . . . Mr. Sfortz! He hasn't screamed or jumped up once . . . and we've been on the air a minute-and-a-half!
Higher!
Freeze!
Higher!
Author, Author!
GETZOFF

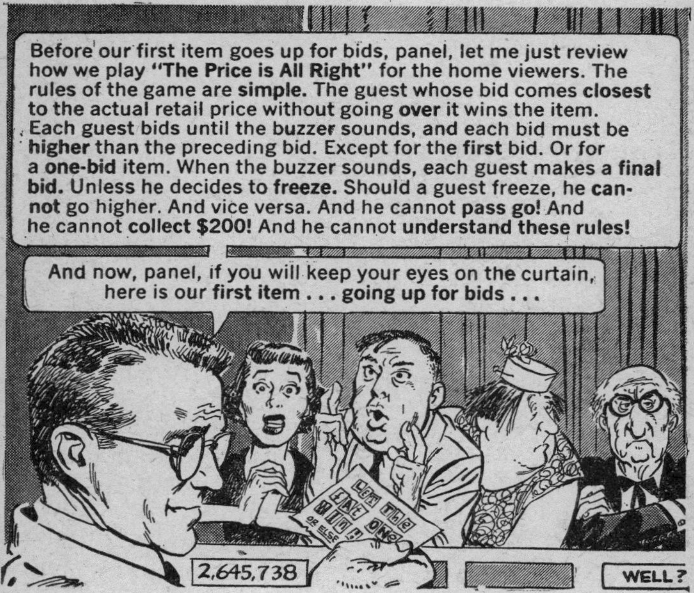
Before our first item goes up for bids, panel, let me just review how we play **"The Price is All Right"** for the home viewers. The rules of the game are **simple.** The guest whose bid comes **closest** to the actual retail price without going **over** it wins the item. Each guest bids until the buzzer sounds, and each bid must be **higher** than the preceding bid. Except for the **first** bid. Or for a **one-bid** item. When the buzzer sounds, each guest makes a **final bid.** Unless he decides to **freeze.** Should a guest freeze, he **cannot** go higher. And vice versa. And he cannot **pass go!** And he cannot **collect $200!** And he cannot **understand these rules!**
And now, panel, if you will keep your eyes on the curtain, here is our **first item . . . going up for bids . . .**
Let the fat one win! OR ELSE
2,645,738
WELL?

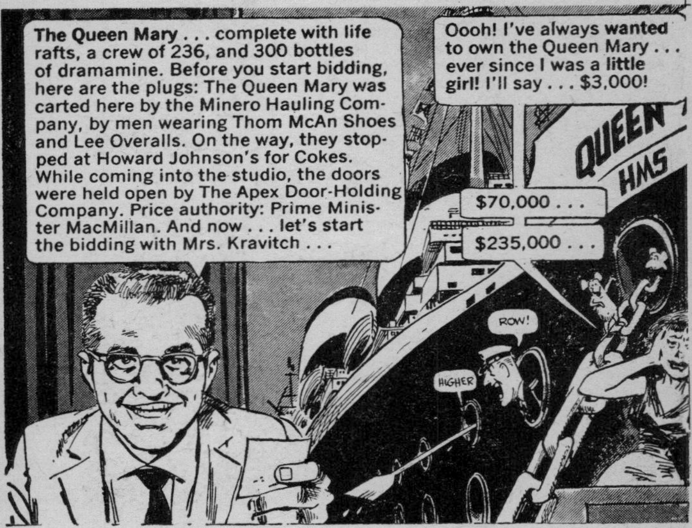
The Queen Mary . . . complete with life rafts, a crew of 236, and 300 bottles of dramamine. Before you start bidding, here are the plugs: The Queen Mary was carted here by the Minero Hauling Company, by men wearing Thom McAn Shoes and Lee Overalls. On the way, they stopped at Howard Johnson's for Cokes. While coming into the studio, the doors were held open by The Apex Door-Holding Company. Price authority: Prime Minister MacMillan. And now . . . let's start the bidding with Mrs. Kravitch . . .
Oooh! I've always wanted to own the Queen Mary . . . ever since I was a little girl! I'll say . . . $3,000!
$70,000 . . .
$235,000 . . .
QUEEN
HMS
ROW!
HIGHER

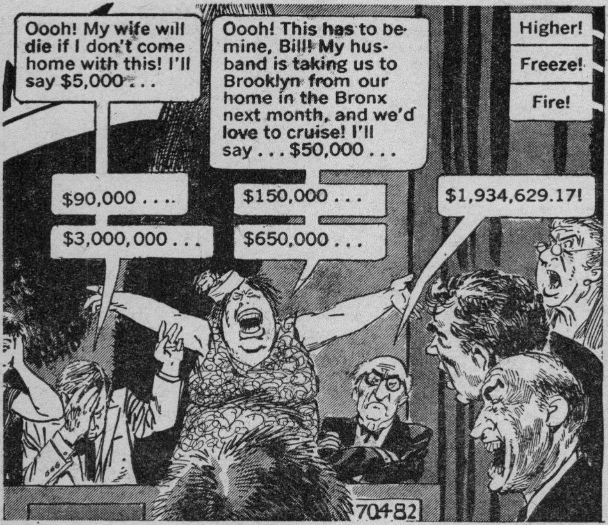
Oooh! My wife will die if I don't come home with this! I'll say $5,000 . . .
Oooh! This has to be mine, Bill! My husband is taking us to Brooklyn from our home in the Bronx next month, and we'd love to cruise! I'll say . . . $50,000 . . .
Higher!
Freeze!
Fire!
$90,000 . . . .
$3,000,000 . . .
$150,000 . . .
$650,000 . . .
$1,934,629.17!
70482

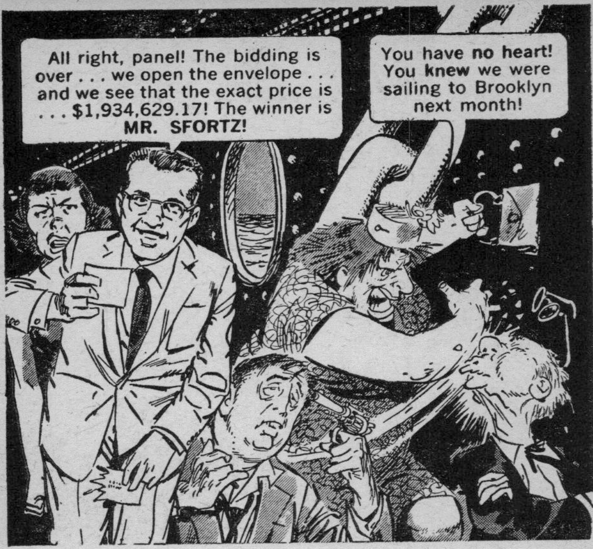
All right, panel! The bidding is over . . . we open the envelope . . . and we see that the exact price is . . . $1,934,629.17! The winner is **MR. SFORTZ!**
You have **no heart!** You **knew** we were sailing to Brooklyn next month!

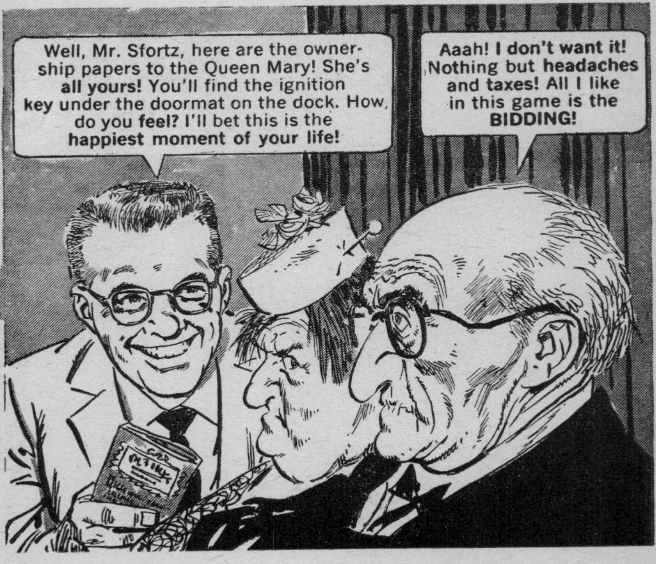
Well, Mr. Sfortz, here are the ownership papers to the Queen Mary! She's **all yours!** You'll find the ignition key under the doormat on the dock. How do you **feel?** I'll bet this is the **happiest moment of your life!**
Aaah! **I don't want it!** Nothing but **headaches** and **taxes!** All I like in this game is the **BIDDING!**

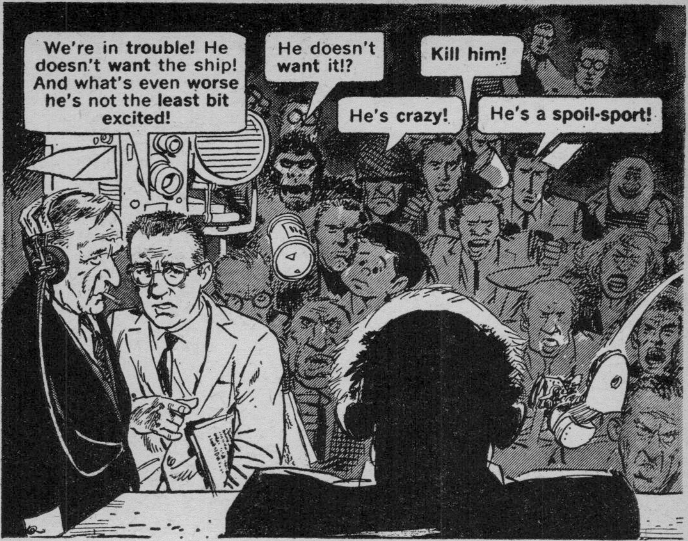
We're in trouble! He doesn't want the ship! And what's even worse he's not the least bit excited!
He doesn't want it!?
Kill him!
He's crazy!
He's a spoil-sport!

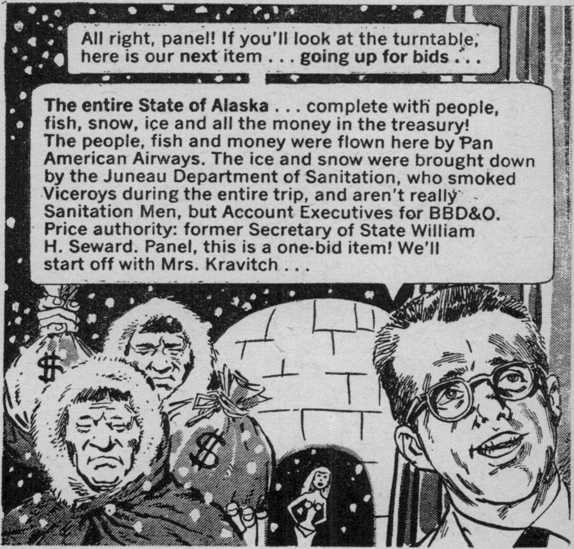
All right, panel! If you'll look at the turntable, here is our next item . . . going up for bids . . .
The entire State of Alaska . . . complete with people, fish, snow, ice and all the money in the treasury! The people, fish and money were flown here by Pan American Airways. The ice and snow were brought down by the Juneau Department of Sanitation, who smoked Viceroys during the entire trip, and aren't really Sanitation Men, but Account Executives for BBD&O. Price authority: former Secretary of State William H. Seward. Panel, this is a one-bid item! We'll start off with Mrs. Kravitch . . .

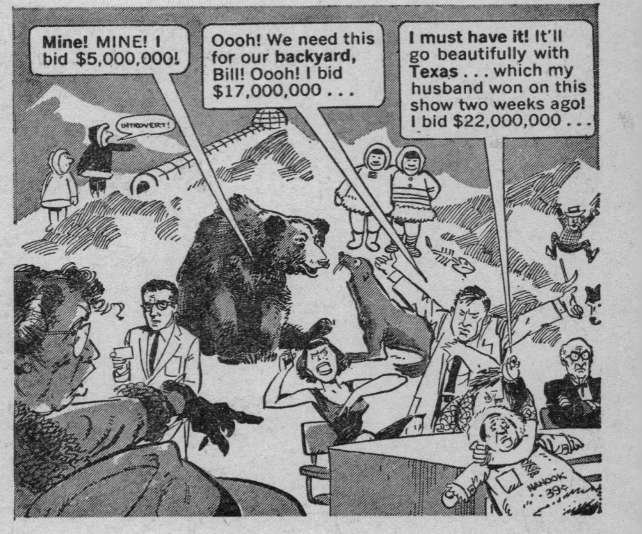
**Mine!** MINE! I bid $5,000,000!
INTROVERT!
Oooh! We need this for our **backyard,** Bill! Oooh! I bid $17,000,000 . . .
**I must have it!** It'll go beautifully with **Texas** . . . which my husband won on this show two weeks ago! I bid $22,000,000 . . .
NANOOK 39¢

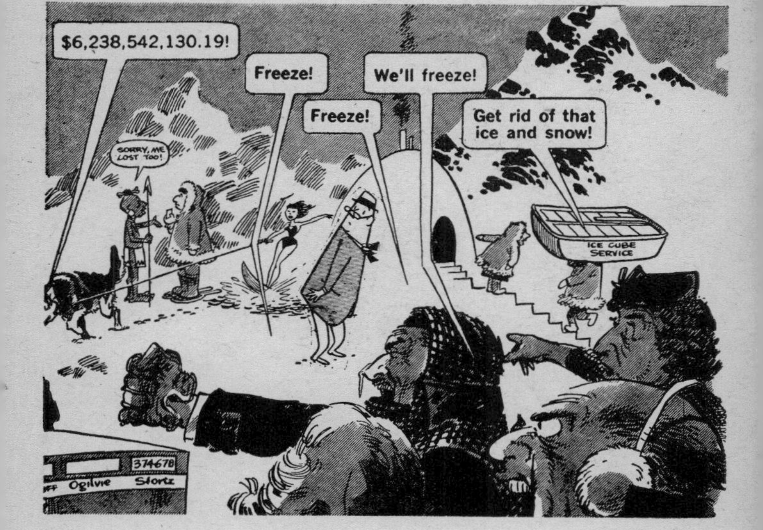
$6,238,542,130.19!
SORRY, ME LOST TOO!
Freeze!
Freeze!
We'll freeze!
Get rid of that ice and snow!
ICE CUBE SERVICE
374678
Ogilvie
Stortz

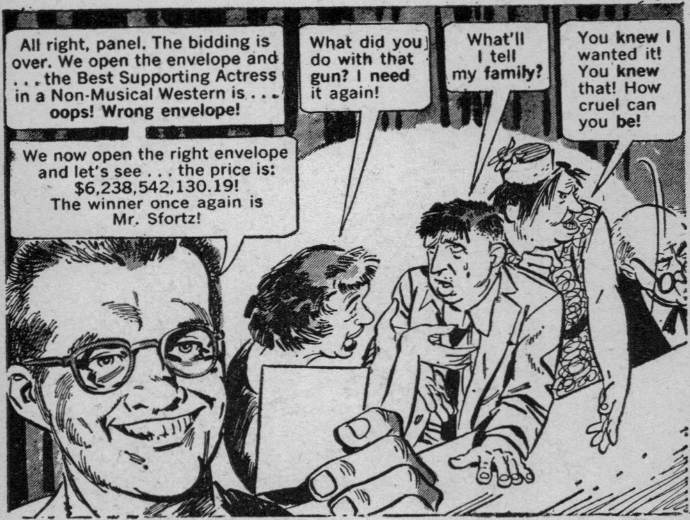
All right, panel. The bidding is over. We open the envelope and . . . the Best Supporting Actress in a Non-Musical Western is . . . oops! Wrong envelope!
We now open the right envelope and let's see . . . the price is: $6,238,542,130.19! The winner once again is Mr. Sfortz!
What did you do with that gun? I need it again!
What'll I tell my family?
You knew I wanted it! You knew that! How cruel can you be!

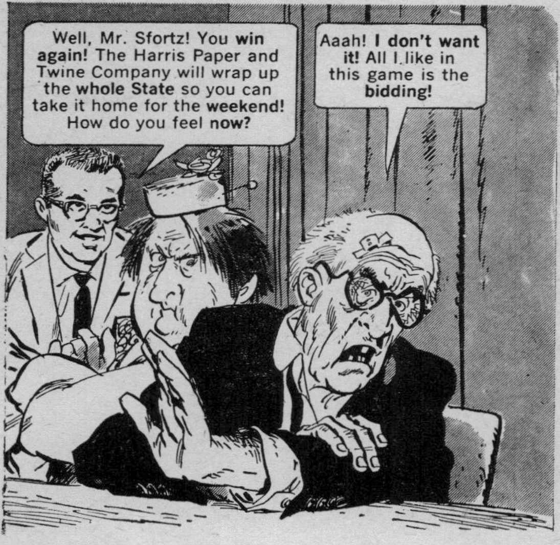
Well, Mr. Sfortz! You win again! The Harris Paper and Twine Company will wrap up the whole State so you can take it home for the weekend! How do you feel now?
Aaah! I don't want it! All I like in this game is the bidding!

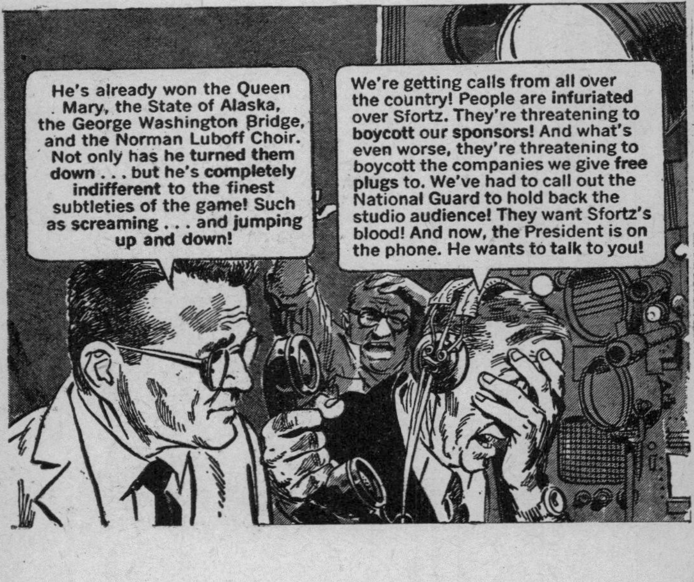
He's already won the Queen Mary, the State of Alaska, the George Washington Bridge, and the Norman Luboff Choir. Not only has he turned them down . . . but he's completely indifferent to the finest subtleties of the game! Such as screaming . . . and jumping up and down!
We're getting calls from all over the country! People are infuriated over Sfortz. They're threatening to boycott our sponsors! And what's even worse, they're threatening to boycott the companies we give free plugs to. We've had to call out the National Guard to hold back the studio audience! They want Sfortz's blood! And now, the President is on the phone. He wants to talk to you!

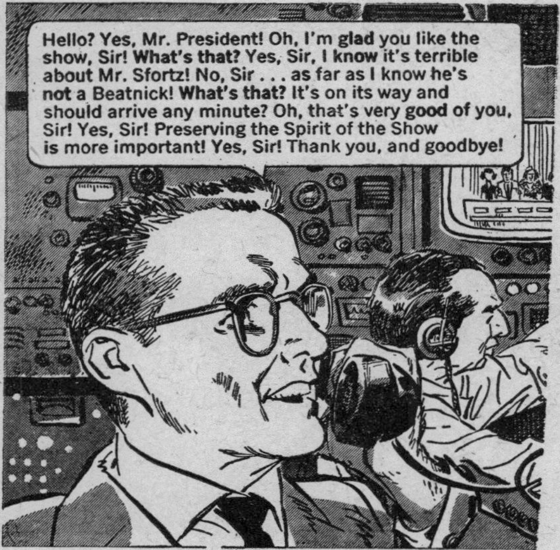
Hello? Yes, Mr. President! Oh, I'm glad you like the show, Sir! What's that? Yes, Sir, I know it's terrible about Mr. Sfortz! No, Sir . . . as far as I know he's not a Beatnick! What's that? It's on its way and should arrive any minute? Oh, that's very good of you, Sir! Yes, Sir! Preserving the Spirit of the Show is more important! Yes, Sir! Thank you, and goodbye!

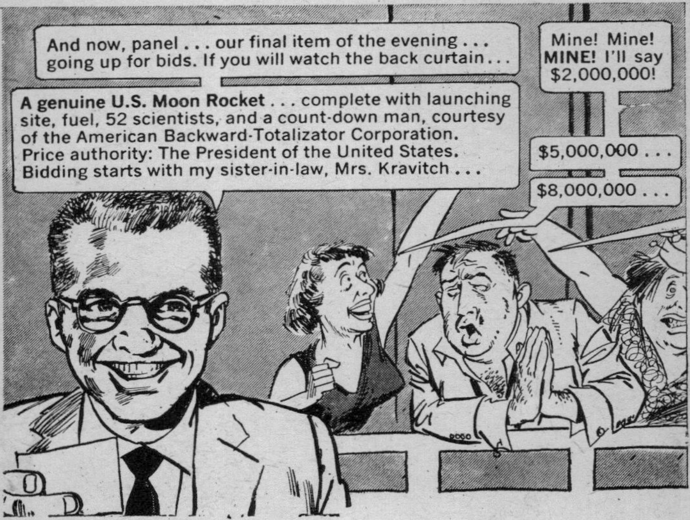
And now, panel . . . our final item of the evening . . . going up for bids. If you will watch the back curtain . . .
A genuine U.S. Moon Rocket . . . complete with launching site, fuel, 52 scientists, and a count-down man, courtesy of the American Backward-Totalizator Corporation. Price authority: The President of the United States. Bidding starts with my sister-in-law, Mrs. Kravitch . . .
Mine! Mine! MINE! I'll say $2,000,000!
$5,000,000 . . .
$8,000,000 . . .

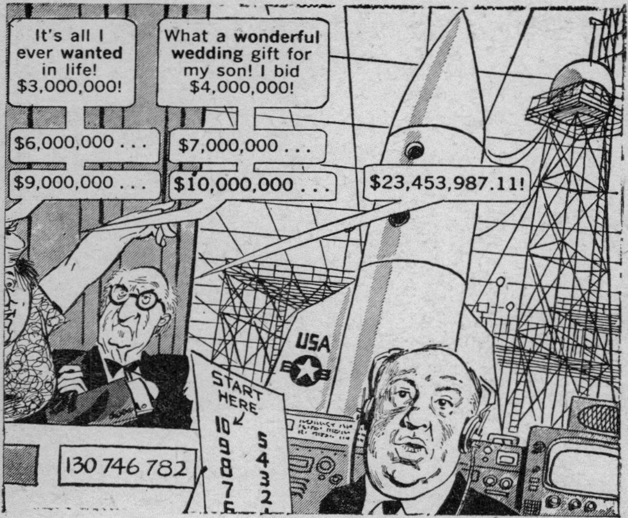
It's all I ever **wanted** in life! $3,000,000!
What a **wonderful wedding** gift for my son! I bid $4,000,000!
$6,000,000 . . .
$7,000,000 . . .
$9,000,000 . . .
$10,000,000 . . .
$23,453,987.11!
USA
START HERE
10 9 8 7 6
5 4 3 2
130 746 782

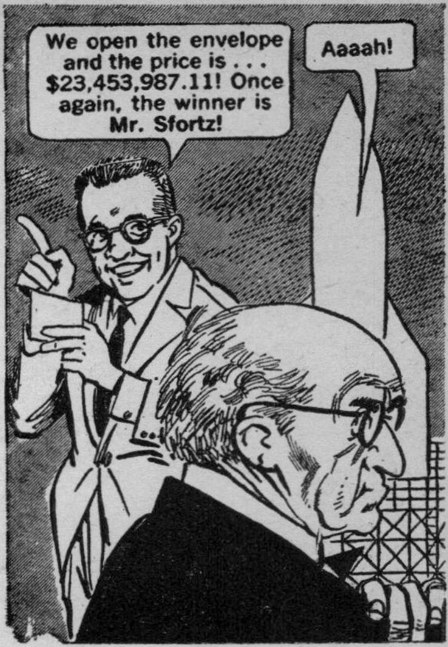
We open the envelope and the price is . . . $23,453,987.11! Once again, the winner is Mr. Sfortz!
Aaaah!

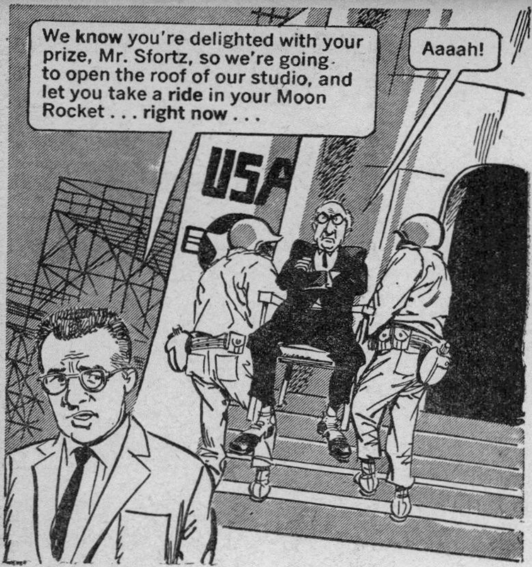
We know you're delighted with your prize, Mr. Sfortz, so we're going to open the roof of our studio, and let you take a ride in your Moon Rocket . . . right now . . .
Aaaah!
USA

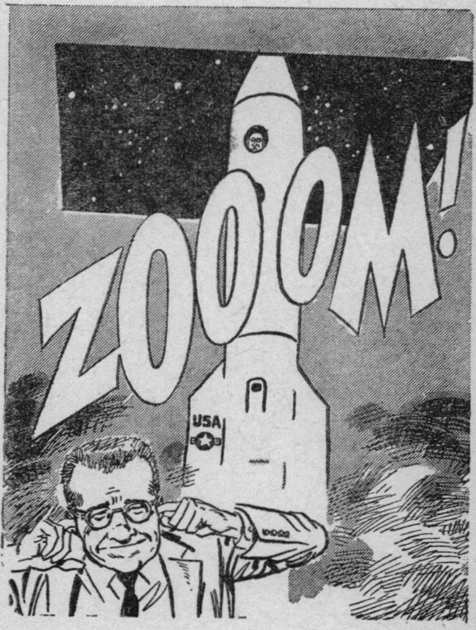
ZOOOM!
USA

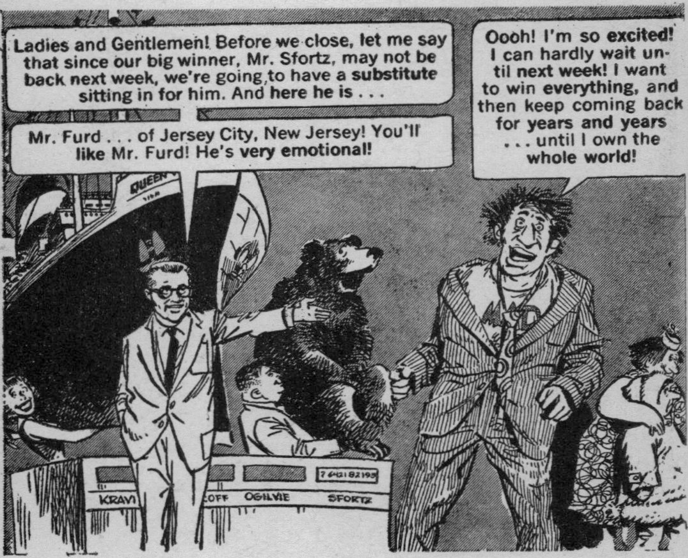
Ladies and Gentlemen! Before we close, let me say that since our big winner, Mr. Sfortz, may not be back next week, we're going to have a substitute sitting in for him. And here he is . . .
Mr. Furd . . . of Jersey City, New Jersey! You'll like Mr. Furd! He's very emotional!
Oooh! I'm so excited! I can hardly wait until next week! I want to win everything, and then keep coming back for years and years . . . until I own the whole world!
KRAVI
OFF
OGILVIE
SFORTZ

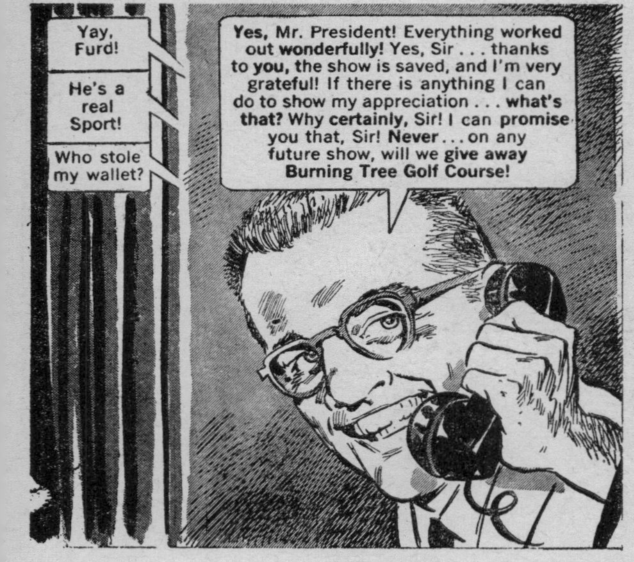
Yay, Furd!
He's a real Sport!
Who stole my wallet?
Yes, Mr. President! Everything worked out wonderfully! Yes, Sir . . . thanks to you, the show is saved, and I'm very grateful! If there is anything I can do to show my appreciation . . . what's that? Why certainly, Sir! I can promise you that, Sir! Never . . . on any future show, will we give away Burning Tree Golf Course!

**END**

And now, Don Martin tells us of his happiest childhood experience...

# ON THE BEACH

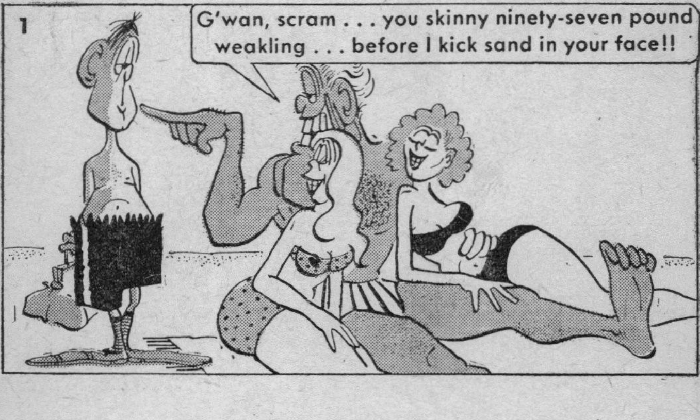
1
G'wan, scram . . . you skinny ninety-seven pound weakling . . . before I kick sand in your face!!

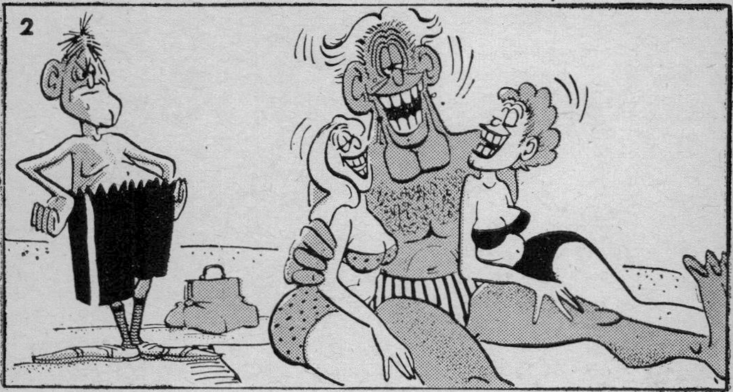

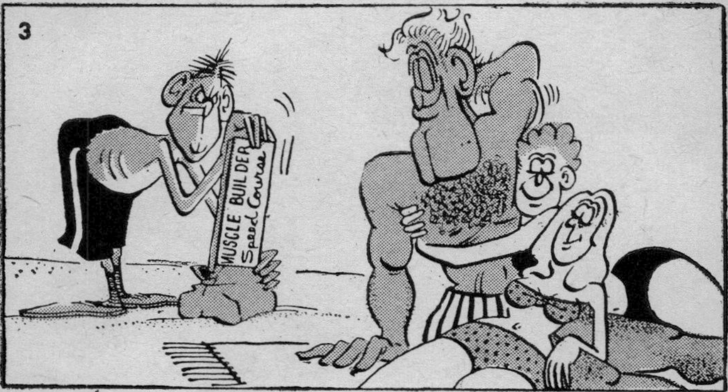
MUSCLE BUILDER
Speed Course

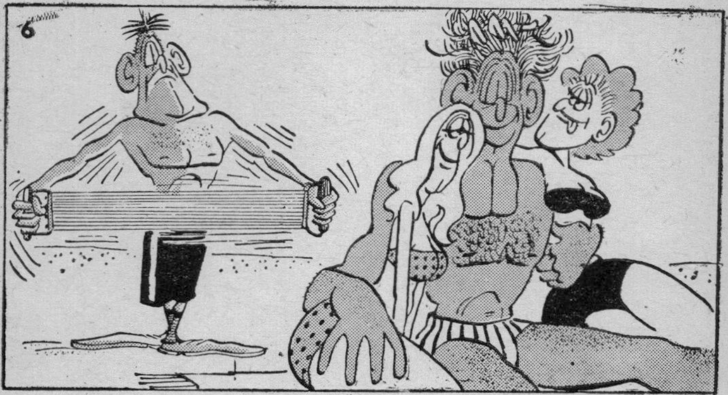
6

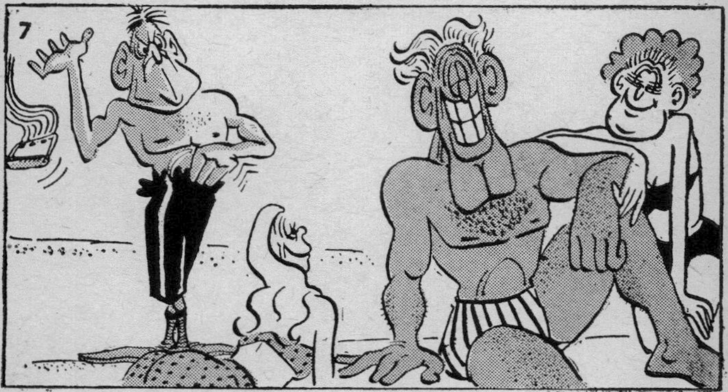
7

**END**

**MAD COMES TO THE DEFENSE OF OUR
MUCH-MALIGNED
YOUNG PEOPLE WITH
THIS SURVEY WHICH REVEALS...**

# WHAT OUR TEENAGERS REALLY THINK ABOUT

Most adults assume
that all teenage girls
ever think about is *boys!*

# THIS IS NOT TRUE!

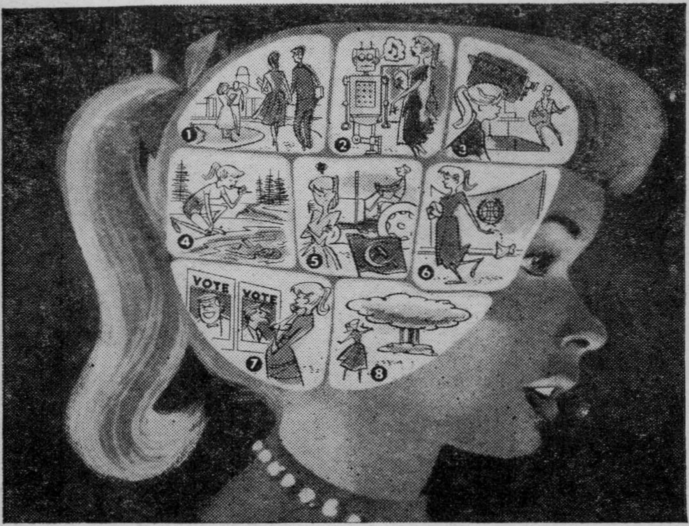
VOTE
VOTE

Actually, teenage girls think about important things like national, international, scientific and cultural problems of today, such as:

## 1 SEGREGATION

A teenage girl thinks about segregation in schools, for it's no fun in classes where boys and girls are separated.

## 2 AUTOMATION

A teenage girl worries about automation because she would hate to see somebody invent a machine to replace a boy.

## 3 ELECTRONICS

A teenage girl is interested in electronics because where else but on TV can she see all those cute boy singers?

## 4 NATURAL RESOURCES

A teenage girl is anxious about the development of her natural resources so all the boys will begin noticing her.

## 5 COMMUNISM

A teenage girl is opposed to Communism because she'd hate living where boys think more of their tractors than of girls.

## 6 UNITED NATIONS

A teenage girl supports the United Nations because she knows that boys from other countries can be cute, too.

## 7 POLITICS

A teenage girl is interested in politics because recently there have been really cute fellers running for office.

## 8 THE ATOMIC BOMB

A teenage girl is concerned about the atomic bomb as a weapon of destruction since it could wipe out all boys.

Most adults assume
that all teenage boys
ever think about is *girls!*

# THIS IS NOT TRUE!

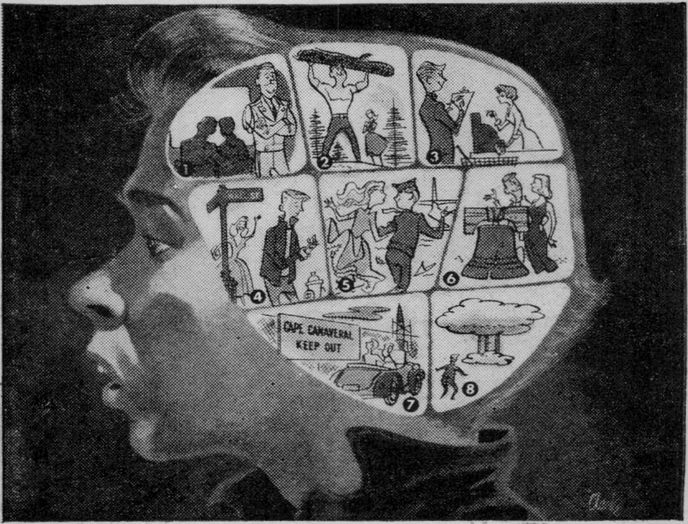
CAPE CANAVERAL
KEEP OUT

Actually, teenage boys think about important things like national, international, scientific and cultural problems of today, such as:

**1 SUMMIT CONFERENCES**

A teenage boy thinks about summit conferences like the kind held with girls in the balconies of movie theaters.

**2 UNDEVELOPED AREAS**

A teenage boy is interested in undeveloped areas like building up his biceps and chest to impress the girls.

**3 MARKET RESEARCH**

A teenage boy knows market research can tell him which supermarket check-out girl is the best bet for a date.

**4 MUTUAL FUNDS**

A teenage boy investigates the possibilities of mutual funds, which means getting the girl to go "Dutch treat."

**5 THE DRAFT**

A teenage boy looks out for the draft, because if he can get his girl in one, she'll want him to keep her warm.

**6 LIBERTY**

A teenage boy is concerned with liberty, especially how much he can take with a girl he's got a heavy date with.

**7 SPACE EXPLORATION**

A teenage boy often indulges in space exploration, which means finding a new place to park and neck with his girl.

**8 THE ATOMIC BOMB**

A teenage boy is concerned with the atomic bomb as a weapon of destruction since it could wipe out all girls.

**END**

As far back as we can remember (meaning last week, which is as far back as we can remember), magazines, newspapers, and television have been using "Before" and "After" advertising. These are ads where they show a picture of some clod *before* using a product, and the same clod *after* using the product. Usually, the *after* picture is so phonied up, and the changes

# THE TRUTH ABOUT "BEFORE" AND

are so fantastic, that there's really no connection with the *before* picture they started with. So — because we hate leaving ill-enough alone — we hired a private eye, dressed him in an Ivy League suit, and turned him loose on Madison Avenue. And now, MAD presents the results of his investigation — documentary proof — our unvarnished, unbelievable, and absolutely unnecessary report which reveals ...

# "AFTER"
## ADS

# THE REDUCING COURSE AD

## TYPICAL "BEFORE" PICTURE

**"BEFORE"** photo shows frowsy woman weighing 369 lbs. standing before share-cropper's shack located in poorer section of city garbage dump. Besides being overweight, she suffers from acne, baldness, and taking fuzzy pictures.

# TYPICAL "AFTER" PICTURE

**"AFTER"** photo shows same woman slimmed down to 118 lbs. Potato sack has turned into Dior original, and she's not only lost her weight, she's lost her address. Now stands before $50,000 house with swimming pool and Cadillac.

# MAD REAL "AFTER PICTURE"

**REAL "AFTER"** photo from MAD's file shows woman lost exactly 8 lbs. This just makes potato sack look baggier. Only other change is that share-cropper's shack has begun settling into ooze. So is woman. She's still pretty hefty.

# THE SLEEPING
# PILL AD

## TYPICAL "BEFORE" PICTURE

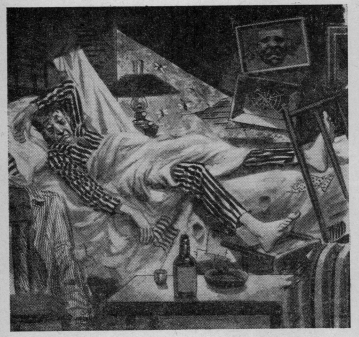

**"BEFORE"** scene shows baggy-eyed man tossing sleeplessly
on rickety bed. His pajamas are wrinkled, the sheets are
torn and dirty, and the room furniture is old and dingy.
It looks like this guy hasn't slept in two or three years.

## TYPICAL "AFTER" PICTURE

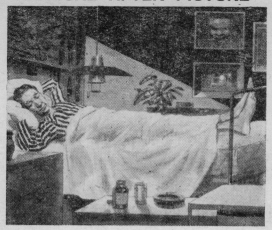

**"AFTER"** scene shows same man sleeping soundly. He now wears silk pajamas, bed has contour sheets, and room is refurnished in Swedish Modern. Sleeping pills' secret ingredient, "pancake make-up", has erased bags under eyes.

## MAD REAL "AFTER PICTURE"

ALFRED E. NEUMAN FOR PRESIDENT
MOXIE

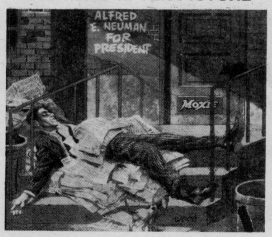

**REAL "AFTER"** scene from MAD's file shows that sleeping pills actually do work. Man fell fast asleep, missed work, got fired, lost mortgaged home, was divorced by his wife, and now spends life sleeping in skid row doorways.

# THE HOME PERMANENT AD

## TYPICAL "BEFORE" PICTURE

**"BEFORE"** picture shows seedy-looking girl wearing seedy-looking dress attending dance in seedy-looking school gym. Friends group around, laughing and jeering at her because she's got drab, lifeless hair. She's miserable and unhappy.

# TYPICAL "AFTER" PICTURE

"AFTER" picture shows same girl at next dance with her new home permanent. She's now a social success. In fact, she's now Queen of England. Gym resembles Westminster Abbey. Friends, led by Sal Mineo, all kneel at her feet.

# MAD REAL "AFTER PICTURE"

REAL "AFTER" picture, from MAD file, shows that home permanents really work. Girl now has beautiful hair. But friends still group around, laughing and jeering at her because now she's got dishpan hands from taking too many.

# THE EYE
# MAKE-UP AD

## TYPICAL "BEFORE" PICTURE

**"BEFORE"** shot shows girl in rags scowling in mirror. She suffers from "no eye make-upitis". The symptoms are obvious. She has wrinkled eyes. She also has a wrinkled forehead, a wrinkled nose, and mainly wrinkled teeth.

## TYPICAL "AFTER" PICTURE

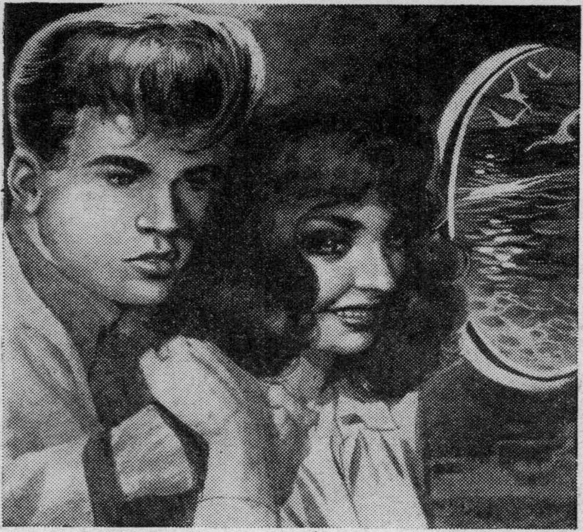

**"AFTER"** shot shows amazing results of eye make-up. Girl has turned into fashion model. Mirror has turned into ships porthole. Mop has turned into Ricky Nelson. Guy who makes eye make-up has turned into millionaire.

## MAD REAL "AFTER PICTURE"

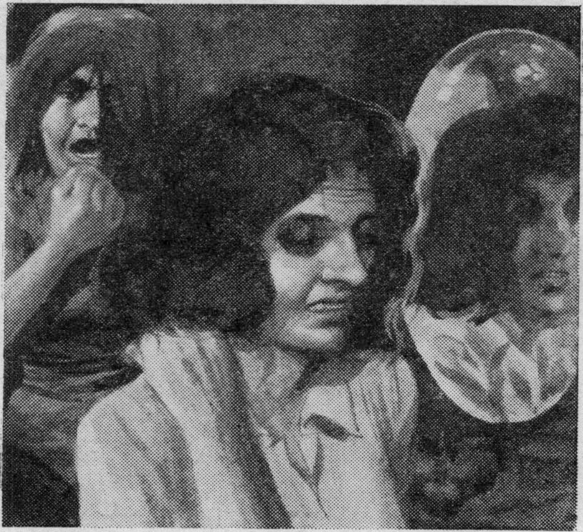

**REAL "AFTER"** shot indicates application of eye make-up has indeed caused change. Girl is still miserable—but now sports two beautiful shiners given to her by an older sister, whose mascara and eye make-up she swiped.

# THE TOOTHPASTE AD

## TYPICAL "BEFORE" PICTURE

**"BEFORE"** scene shows shabby bum who obviously needs a job. Also a bath. Man is suffering from unsightly teeth. Man is also suffering from strange disease which causes concentric rings to emanate from his mouth as he breathes.

# TYPICAL "AFTER" PICTURE

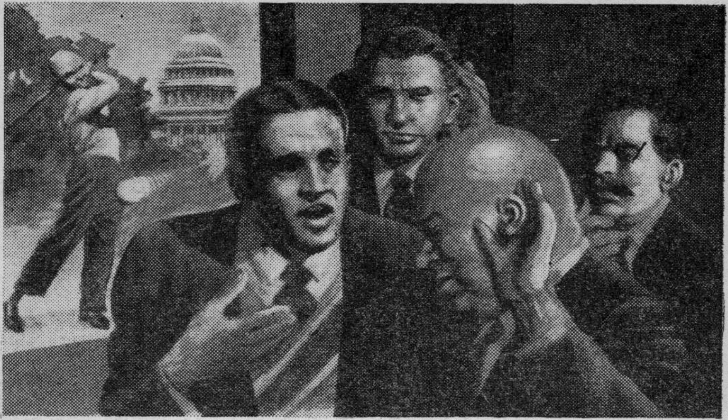

**"AFTER"** scene shows results of single brushing. Teeth sparkle. Man has new suit of clothes, and new job as top State Dept. official, as mouth rings are gone, and protective shield covers teeth, keeping him from talking sense.

# MAD REAL "AFTER PICTURE

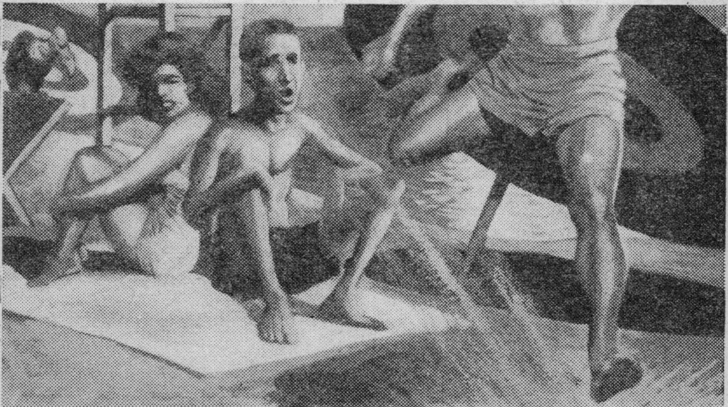

**REAL "AFTER"** scene from MAD file shows that invisible protective shield really prevents decay. It also prevents food from entering mouth, so man starves to point where he ends up as "before" in "I was a 97 pound weakling!" ad.

**END**

# MAD REVEALS INSURMOUNTABLE PROBLEM

## DISCOVERED WHILE

# TESTING CIVILIANS

## FOR

# SPACE FLIGHT

# SPECIAL REPORT

Everyone knows about the intensive Military Space Flight Training Program being carried on by our government, wherein members of our Armed Forces are tested for their abilities to withstand the rigors of Space Flight. But few people are aware of the secret Civilian Space Flight Training Program being carried on by our forward-looking airlines, wherein average people are being tested for their abilities to withstand the rigors of Commercial Space Flight. With this article, MAD now reveals the startling results of the first of these unpublicized Civilian Testing Programs . . .

## AVERAGE CIVILIAN SPACE PASSENGER

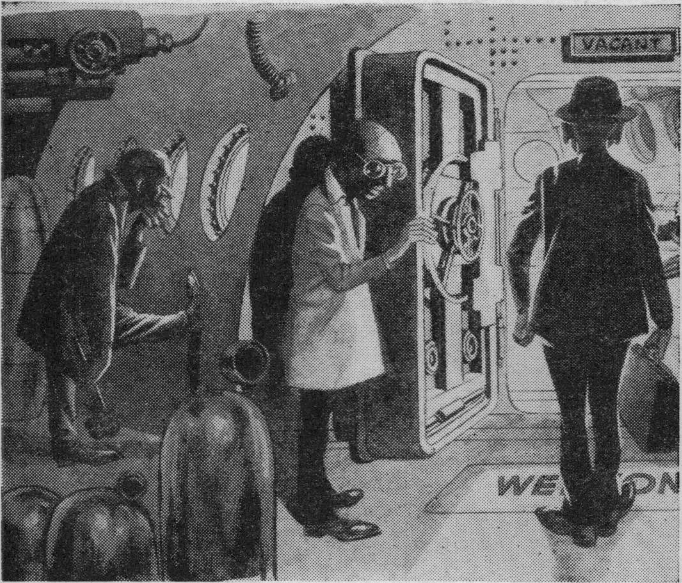
VACANT
WE ON

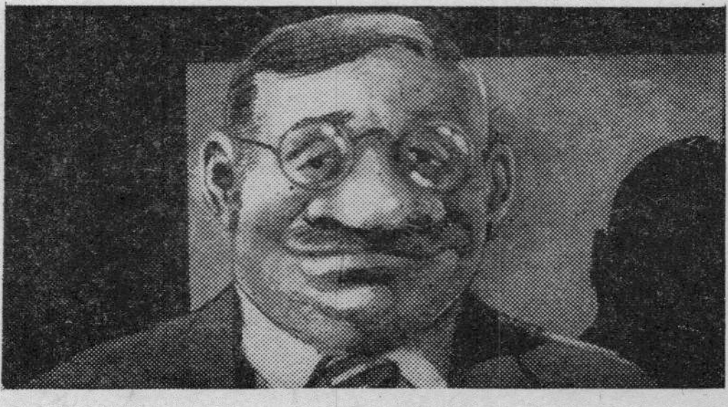

## CAREFULLY SELECTED FOR EXTENSIVE TESTS.

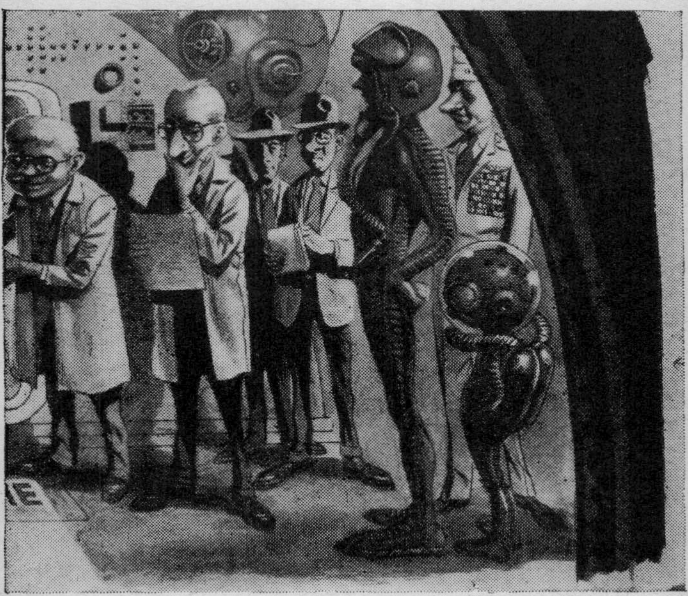

Typical future space flight passenger, Lester B. Cowznofski *(shown above)* being led into Rocket Testing Chamber. Simulated flight into space will show doctors how the average passenger will react to long trip, and reveal problems which may arise.

Mr. Lester B. Cowznofski, average citizen, and first civilian space passenger, *before* tests revealed insurmountable problem.

# MAIN PROBLEM CIVILIAN SPACE TRAVELER FACES

## CAN LESTER B. COWZNOFSKI SURVIVE A LONG PERIOD OF WITHDRAWAL FROM HIS FAMILIAR WAY OF LIFE ON EARTH?

On the theory that the physical rigors of space flight are not the most important problems facing the future civilian space passenger, but rather the mental rigors of having to do without the familiar things he has become accustomed to, Lester B. Cowznofski was sealed in a testing chamber, and subjected to all of the conditions he would face on such a flight. Then, doctors observed how he solved the problem of doing without these familiar things he had to leave behind.

# THESE ARE
# THE FAMILIAR THINGS
# THAT LESTER
# MUST LEAVE BEHIND

### LESTER MUST DO WITHOUT
### HIS LOVING WIFE

For the first time in eight years, they'll be separated.

### LESTER MUST DO WITHOUT
### HIS ADORING CHILDREN

He won't hear their bright gay laughter for a long while.

## LESTER MUST DO WITHOUT
# HIS PERSONAL INTERESTS

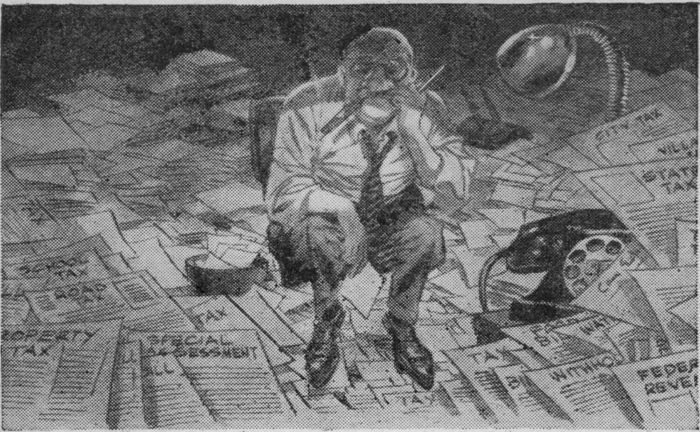
CITY TAX
SCHOOL TAX
TAX
SPECIAL

... the joy of guiding the family ship of state forward.

## LESTER MUST DO WITHOUT
# HIS FAVORITE ENTERTAINMENT

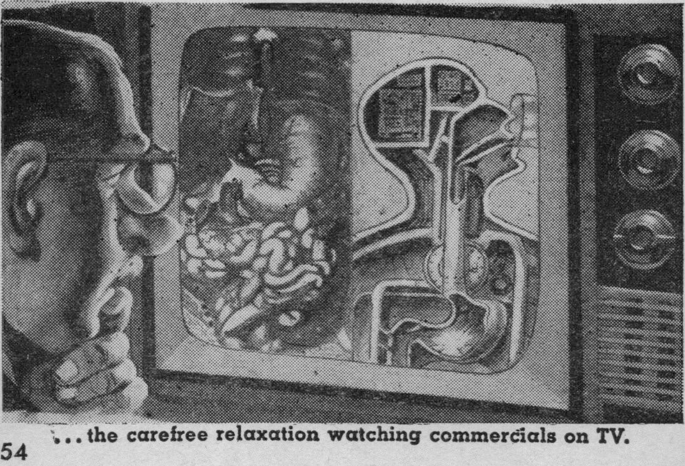

... the carefree relaxation watching commercials on TV.

LESTER MUST DO WITHOUT
## HIS CLOSE FRIENDS

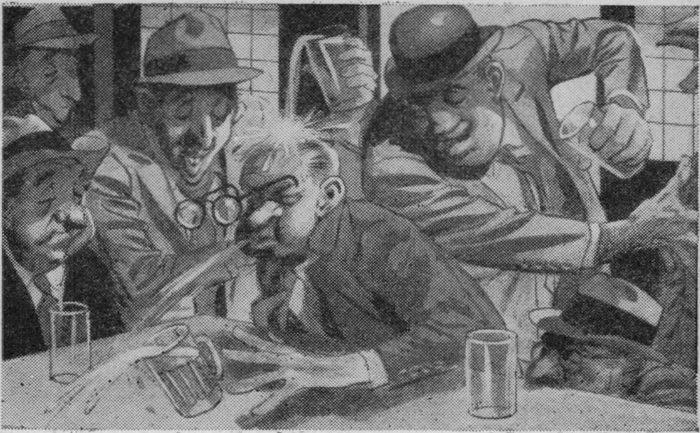

... the gentle fun and heartwarming joy of comradeship.

LESTER MUST DO WITHOUT
## HIS FAMILY OUTINGS

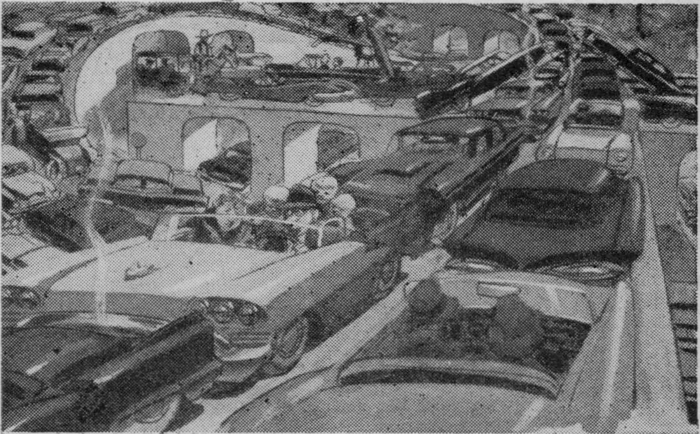

... those relaxing Sunday drives through the countryside.

LESTER MUST DO WITHOUT
## HIS PLEASANT HOBBIES

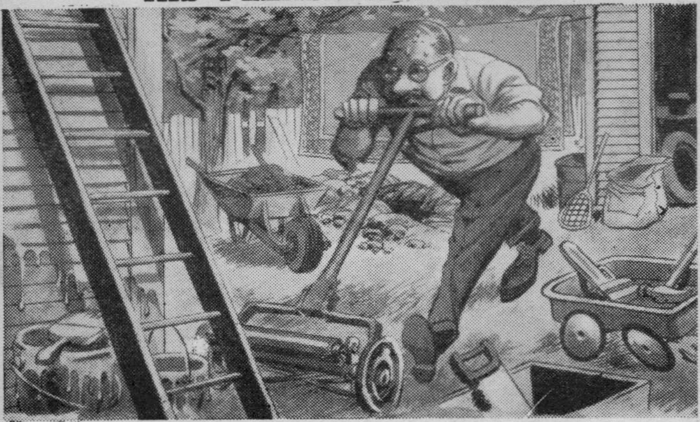

. . . the delightful puttering around the house and garden.

LESTER MUST DO WITHOUT
## HIS LEISURE ACTIVITIES

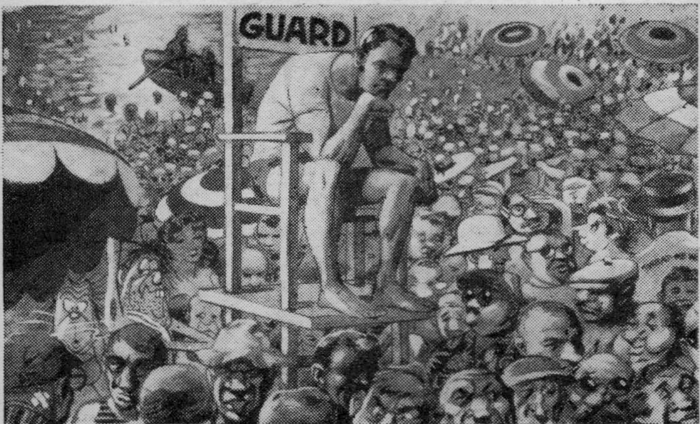
GUARD

. . . the pleasure-filled hours mingling with other folks.

LESTER MUST DO WITHOUT

## HIS AFFECTIONATE RELATIVES

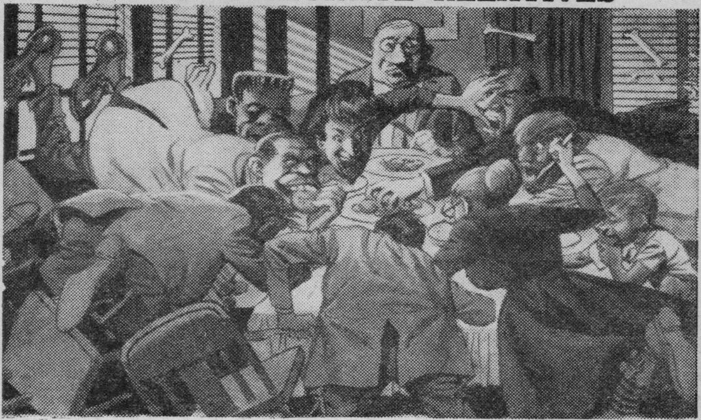

. . . the surprise and pleasure of their unexpected visits.

LESTER MUST DO WITHOUT

## HIS DAILY NEWSPAPERS

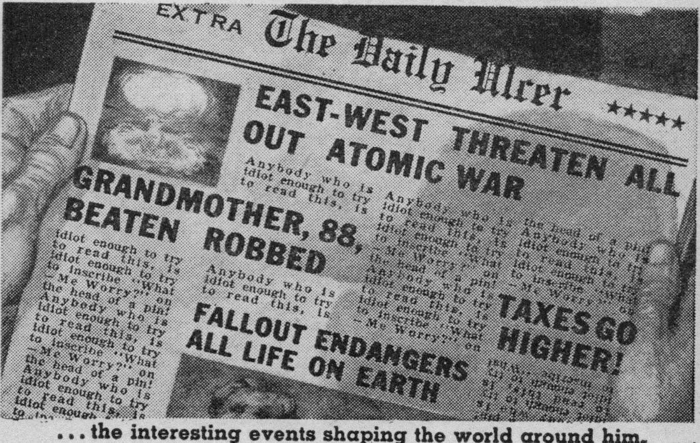
EXTRA
The Daily Ulcer
EAST-WEST THREATEN ALL OUT ATOMIC WAR
Anybody who is idiot enough to try to read this, is
GRANDMOTHER, 88, BEATEN ROBBED
Anybody who is idiot enough to try to read this, is
TAXES GO HIGHER!
FALLOUT ENDANGERS ALL LIFE ON EARTH

. . . the interesting events shaping the world around him.

LESTER MUST DO WITHOUT

## HIS DAILY COMMUTING

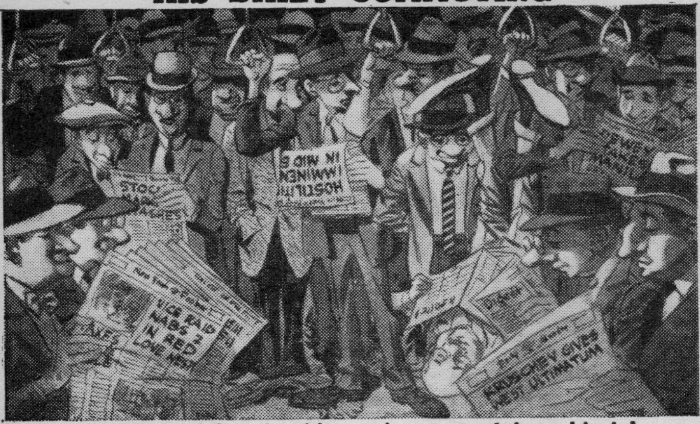
VICE RAID
NABS 2
IN RED
WEST ULTIMATUM

... those restful train rides going to and from his job.

LESTER MUST DO WITHOUT

## HIS HOMECOOKED MEALS

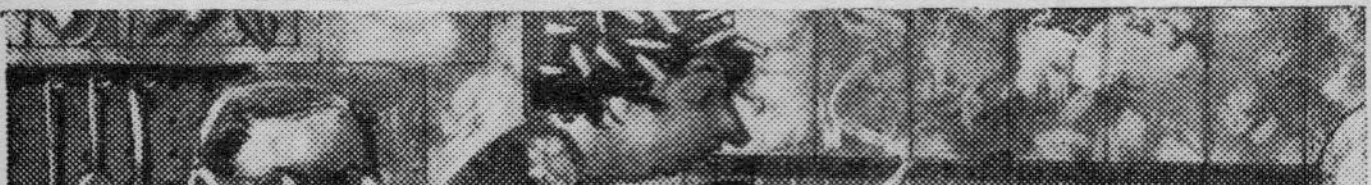
Sports Section

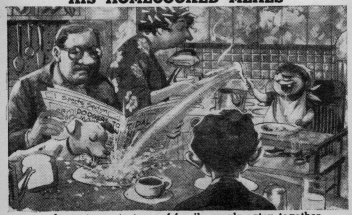

... the tasty, zesty tang of family meals eaten together.

**SURPRISINGLY,
LESTER
MANAGED TO DO
WITHOUT THESE
THINGS NICELY!**

**FOR
INSURMOUNTABLE
PROBLEM DISCOVERED
BY TESTS,
TURN THE PAGE:**

# INSURMO PRO

## HOW TO GET OUT OF THE

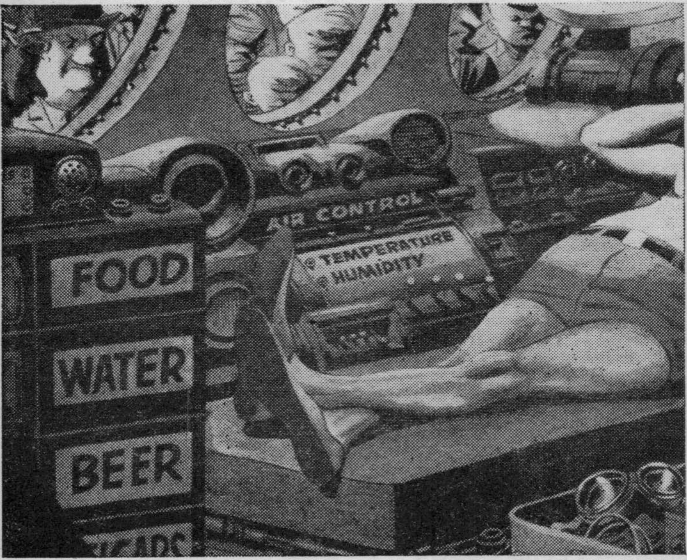
AIR CONTROL
TEMPERATURE
HUMIDITY
FOOD
WATER
BEER

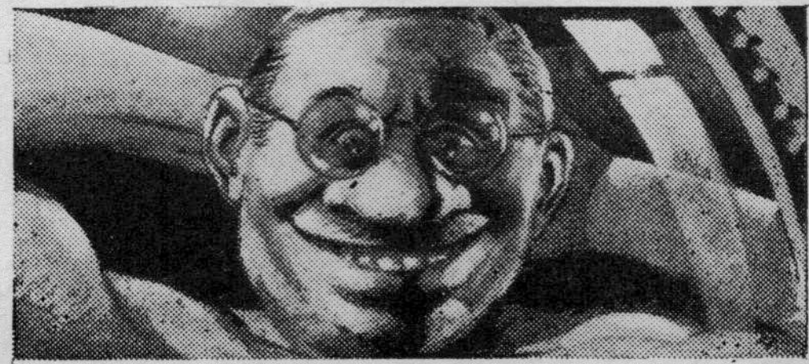

# UNTABLE BLEM

## LESTER COWZNOFSKI TESTING CHAMBER?

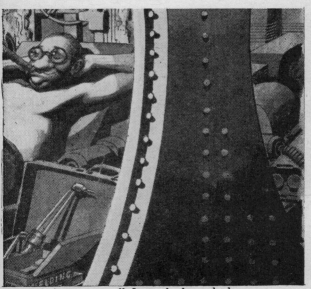

Yes, unbeknownst to all, Lester had sneaked a portable welding outfit into the Rocket Testing Chamber, and sealed himself in permanently. Before severing communication with the outside world, Lester made one brief statement (reprinted below) over the PA system. As MAD goes to press, Lester is still in there.

Mr. Lester B. Cowznofski, the first civilian space passenger: "I'd be crazy to go back to them things I hadda leave behind!"

**END**

# Scenes We'd Like to See

## The Big Break

GOOD LUCK ON OPENING NIGHT!

SUCCESS

M·D

2

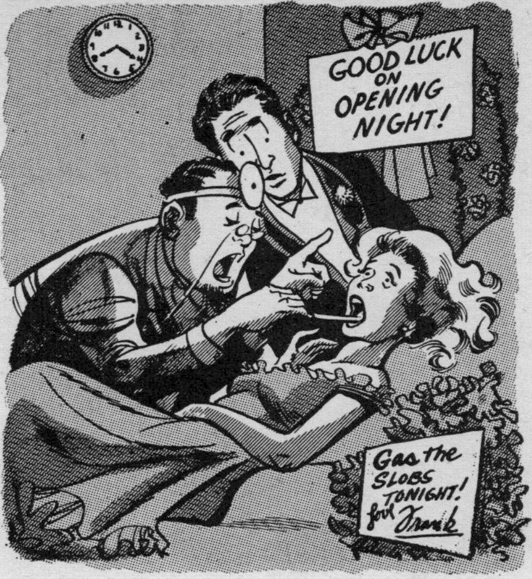
GOOD LUCK ON OPENING NIGHT!
Gas the SLOBS TONIGHT! Frank

3

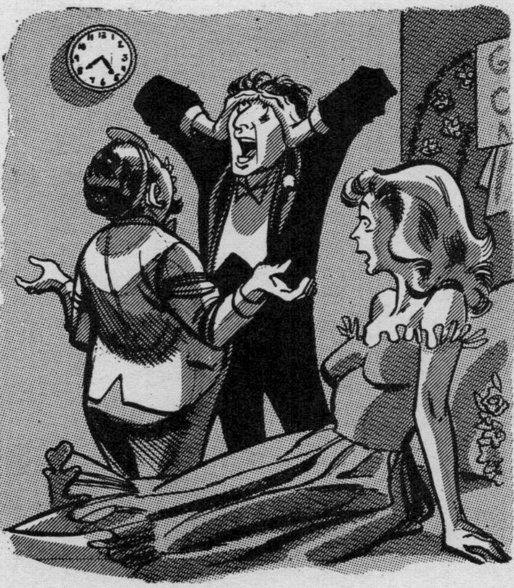

4

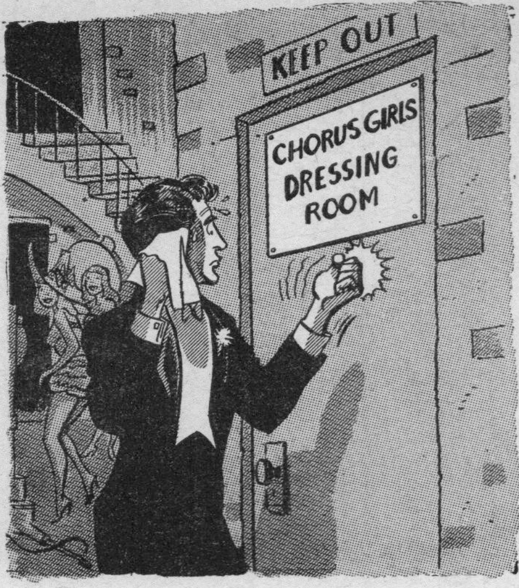
KEEP OUT
CHORUS GIRLS DRESSING ROOM

5

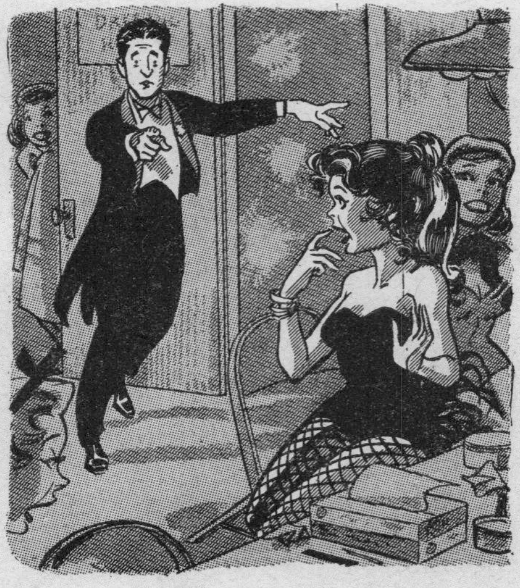

**6**

**7**

END

This is the time of year when thousands of loyal fans stream into hundreds of stadiums all over the country on Saturday afternoons. There, amid pennants and cheers, they scream, yell, and generally behave like idiots for close to three hours. Unfortunately, most of these people watch the field! We say "unfortunately" because they miss the best action . . . namely the action going on around them in the stands. Here, then, is an article explaining how you can enjoy the game of

# GRANDSTAND FOOTBALL

# GRANDSTAND FOOTBALL

## THE ENDS

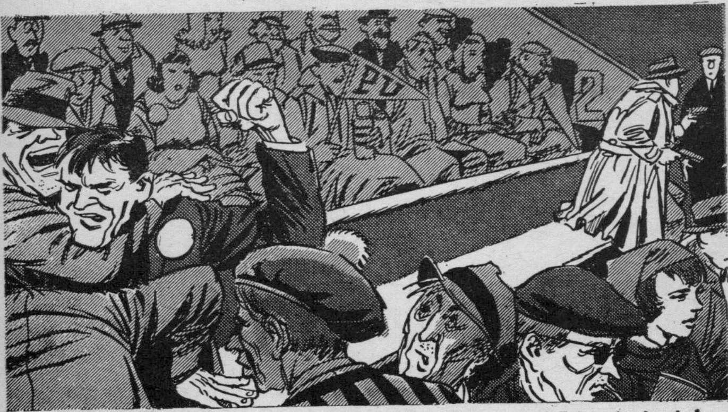

**THE ENDS** are first to arrive at the game. It's their job to protect the line until their teammates arrive by preventing opposition players from grabbing any of the seats in that line.

## THE TACKLES

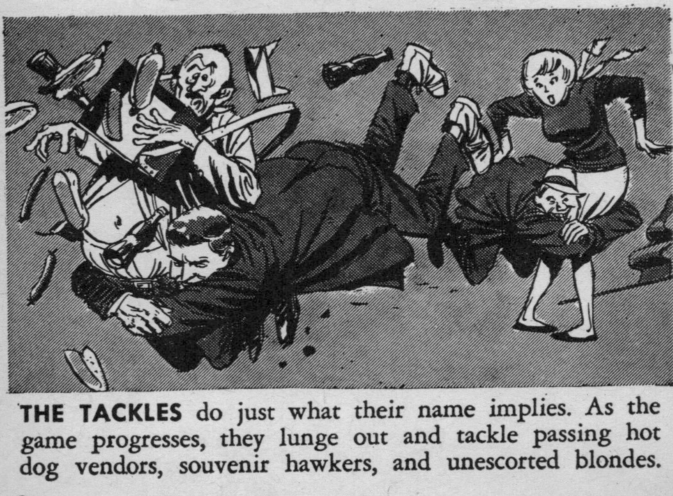

**THE TACKLES** do just what their name implies. As the game progresses, they lunge out and tackle passing hot dog vendors, souvenir hawkers, and unescorted blondes.

# PLAYER POSITIONS

## THE GUARDS

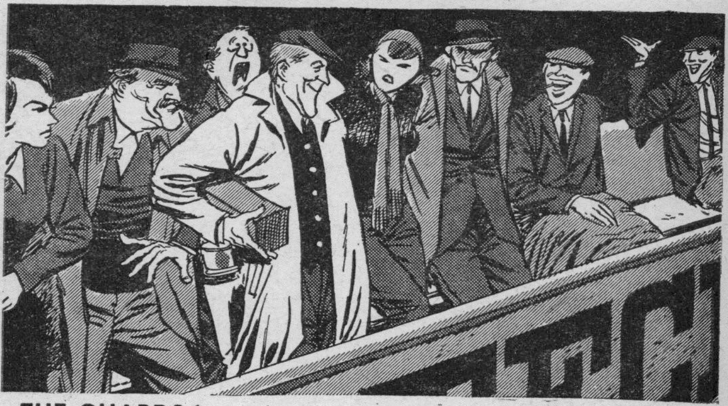

**THE GUARDS** have the important job of guarding the seat of the Center, who somehow always manages to be the last player to arrive, making everybody else in the line stand.

## THE CENTER

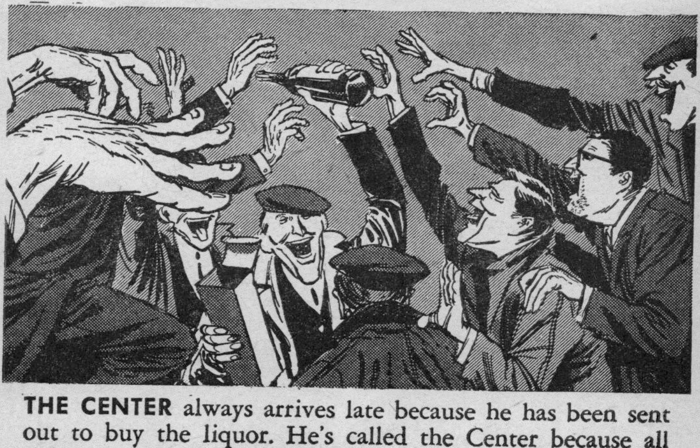

**THE CENTER** always arrives late because he has been sent out to buy the liquor. He's called the Center because all the action centers around him. as he controls the bottle.

# THE QUARTERBACK

**THE QUARTERBACK** takes the bottle directly from the Center, and ends up on his back by the end of a quarter.

# THE HALFBACKS

**THE HALFBACKS** do a little better. They take the bottle when it's passed, and end up on their backs by the half.

# THE FULLBACK

**THE FULLBACK** is a 60 minute man. He usually manages to play out the full game before landing flat on his back.

# GLOSSARY OF GRANDSTAND FOOTBALL TERMS

### CLIPPING

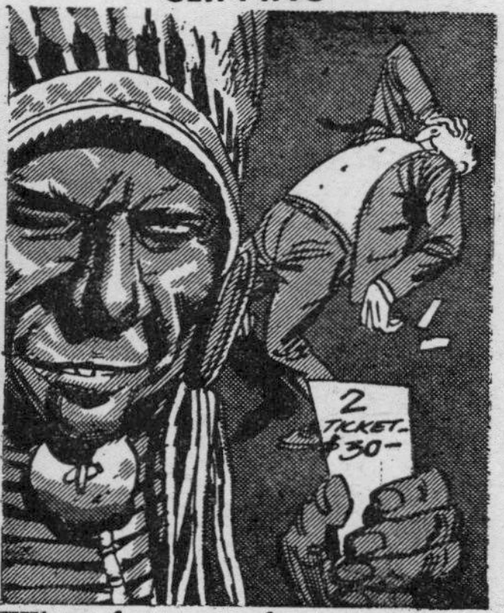
2
TICKET
$30—

What fan gets from a ticket scalper outside the stadium.

### QUARTERBACK SNEAK

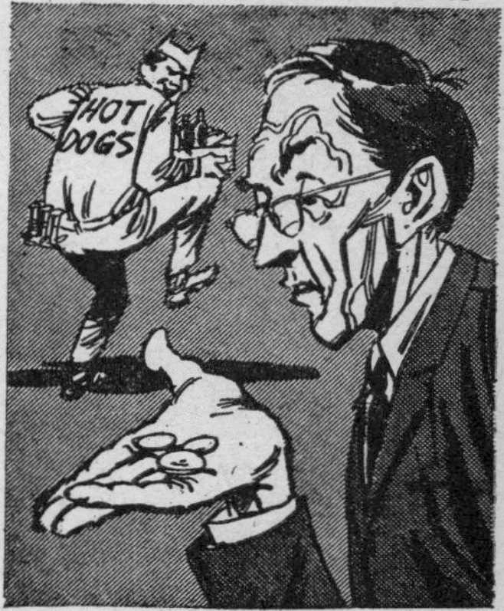
HOT
DOGS

When sneaky hot dog vendor short changes you two-bits.

### ILLEGAL RECEIVER

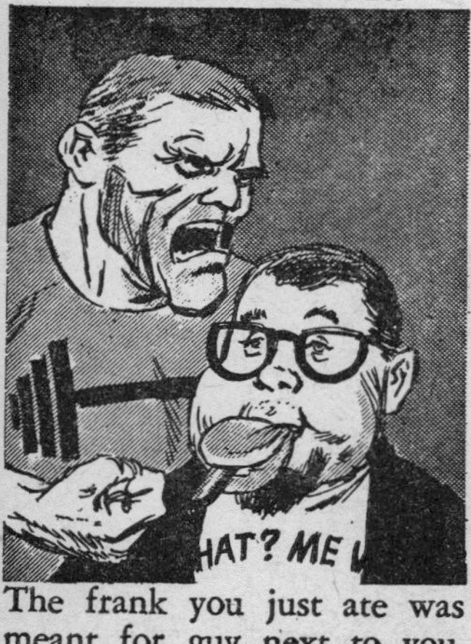
HAT? ME

The frank you just ate was meant for guy next to you.

### INCHES TO GO

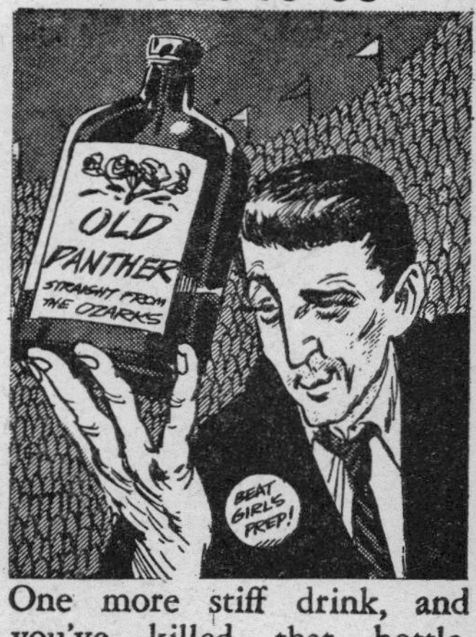
OLD
PANTHER
STRAIGHT FROM
THE OZARKS
BEAT
GIRLS
PREP!

One more stiff drink, and you've killed that bottle.

**BACKFIELD IN MOTION**

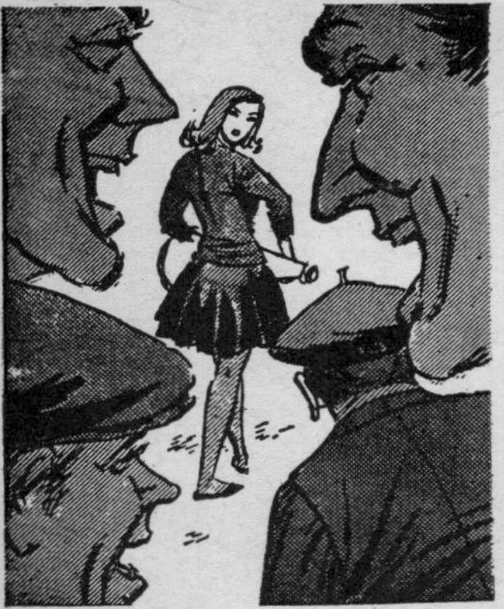

Noticed when a well-shaped cheerleader walks by stands.

**FORWARD PASS**

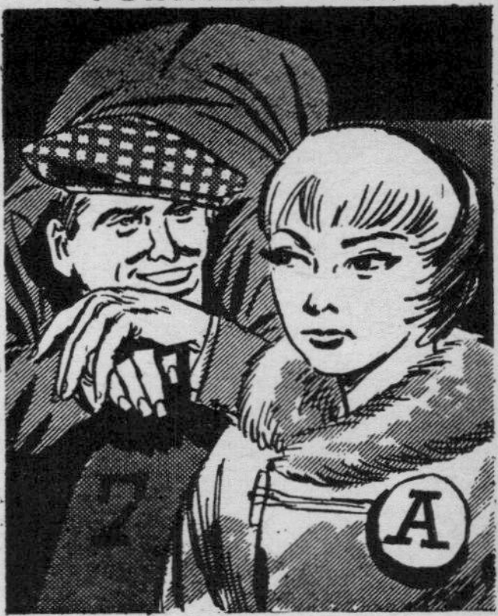
A

Trying to make out with the blonde in the row in front.

**FUMBLE**

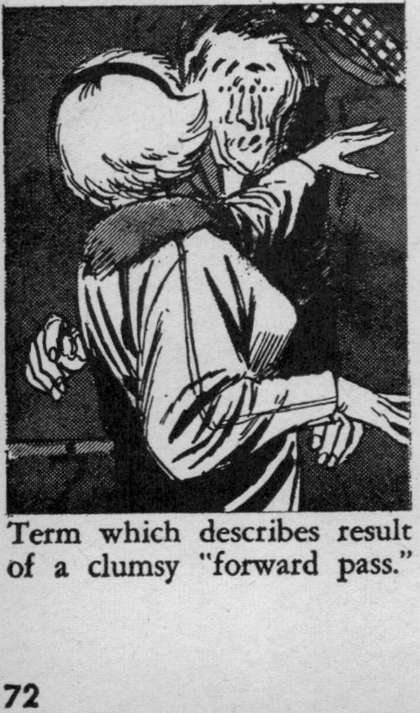

Term which describes result of a clumsy "forward pass."

**LINE-BACKER**

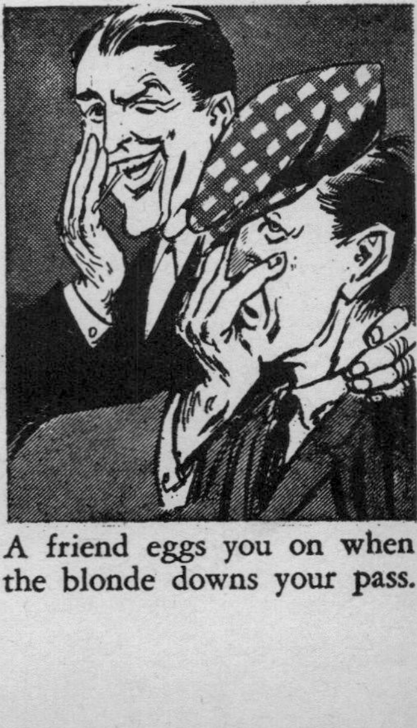

A friend eggs you on when the blonde downs your pass.

**HOLDING**

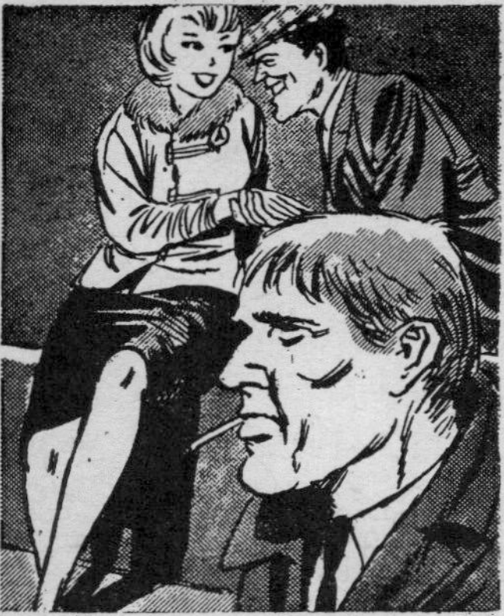

Blonde shares blanket with you after completed pass.

**HUDDLE**

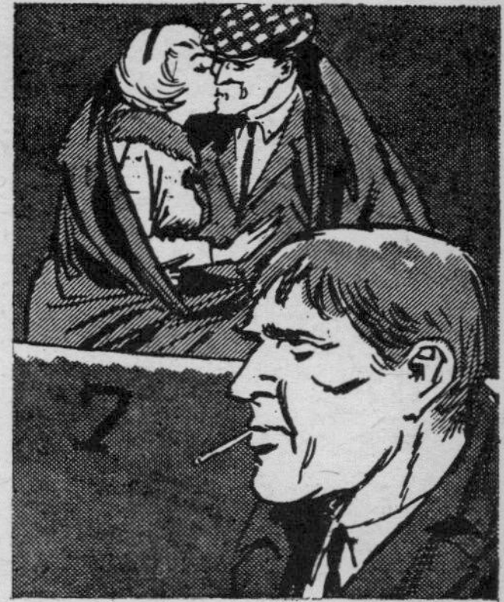

Term which describes result of a completed forward pass.

**PASS INTERFERENCE**

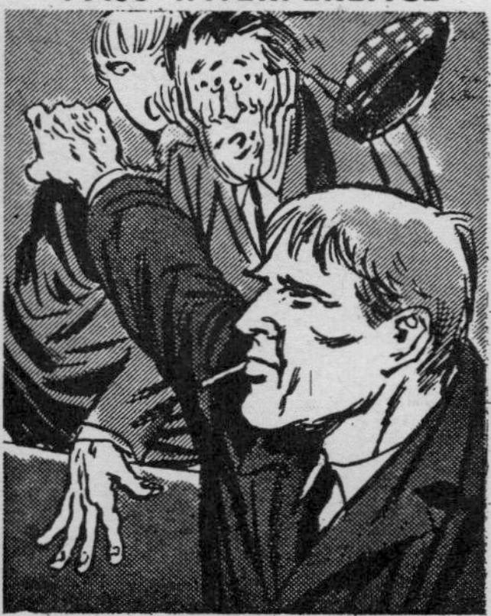

Guy sitting next to blonde turns out to be her husband.

**FOOTBALL**

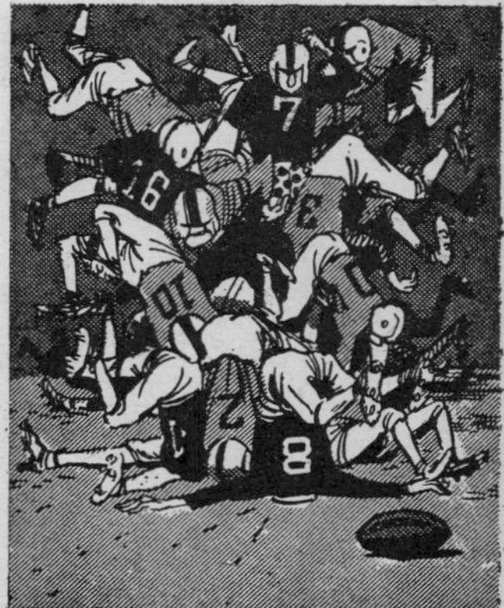

Whatever those 22 clods on the playing field are doing.

# ALL-TIME GRANDSTAND FOOTBALL GREATS

A GALLERY OF GRANDSTAND FOOTBALL HEROES WHO HAVE DISTINGUISHED THEMSELVES DURING PAST FALL CLASSICS BY THEIR COURAGE, STAMINA, AND ALCOHOLIC CONTENT

## MONROE FERNFEATHER
Army '39

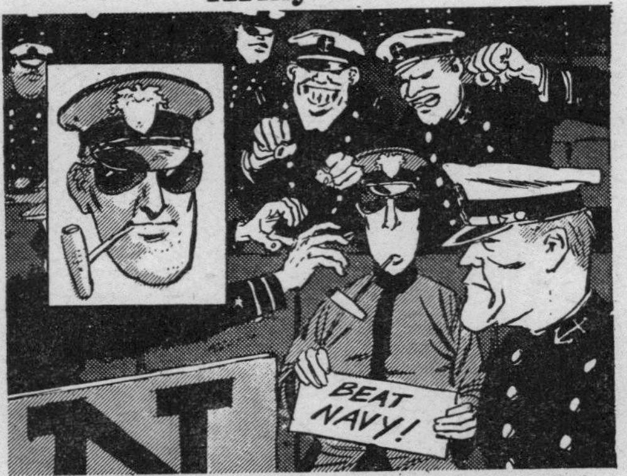
BEAT NAVY!

During Army-Navy game in 1938, Cadet Fernfeather became first Army man to sit through both halfs in Navy cheering section. Was given full Military Funeral, and graduated posthumously.

## DELBERT (BIFF) SMEED
### Nebraska '51

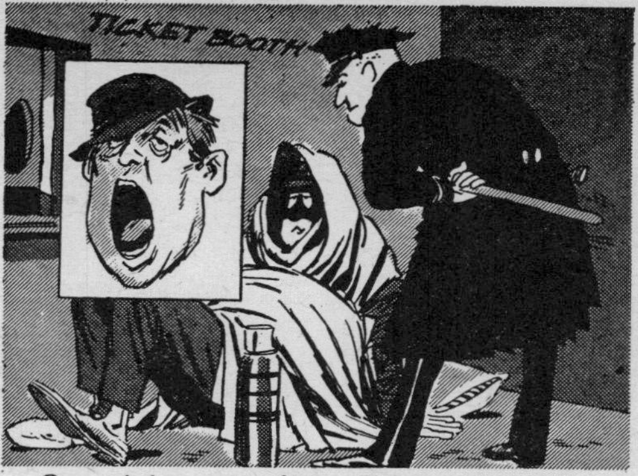
TICKET BOOTH

On night preceding Kansas-Nebraska game, Smeed slept outside Nebraska stadium, waiting for ticket booth to open, only to discover next morning that game was being played at Kansas.

## SPENCER (GO-GO) McNULTY
### UCLA '46

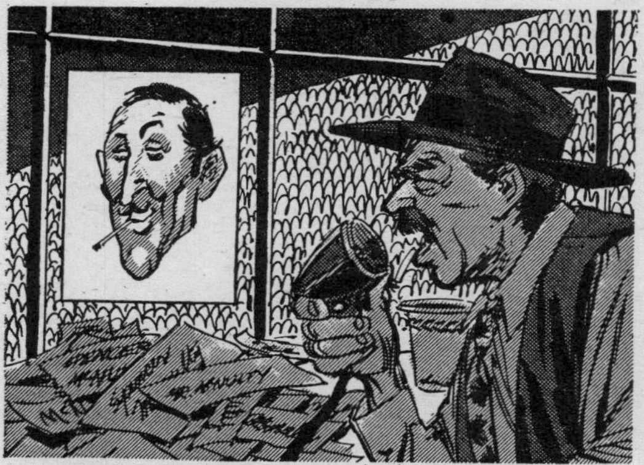

"Go-Go" McNulty set all-time Pacific Coast Conference record during the UCLA-Southern California game back in 1944 by having himself paged 47 times over the public address system.

## BEAUREGARD FINSTER
### Tulane '45

Finster set Southeastern Conference record during Georgia Tech — Tulane game in 1944 by stomping down on 74 consecutive empty Coca-Cola cups, producing a loud "POP" every time.

## ARDSLEY WAXWING
### SMU '53

Waxwing won his laurels during the Texas Christian — Southern Methodist game in 1952 when he tore down the TCU goalposts singlehanded, before learning the game was only half over.

## BARNEY (RAH-RAH) WINDLASS
### Iowa '55

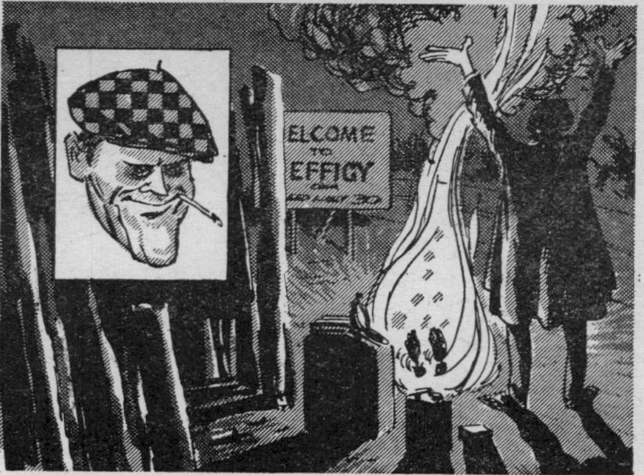
ELCOME
TO
EFFIGY

Windlass became a Grandstand Great when he was barred from all scheduled Iowa games during 1953 for burning the Iowa coach in Effigy, which is a small town just outside Iowa City.

## KYLE ESTERHAZY
### Penn State '13

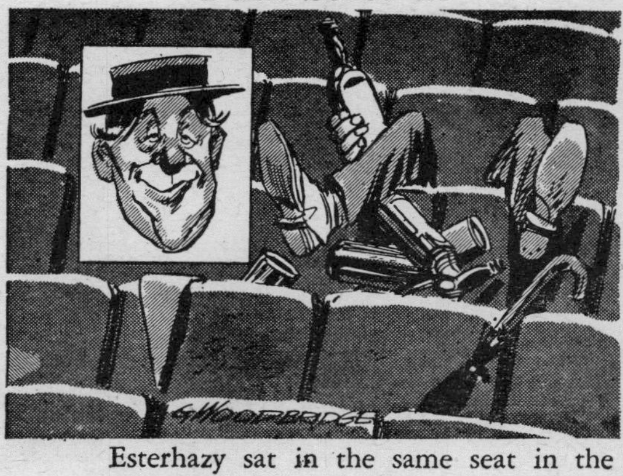

Esterhazy sat in the same seat in the same row in the same section of the stadium for 211 consecutive Penn State home games without once being sober enough to see what was going on.

## BARCLAY BRISK
### Notre Dame '24

Barclay Brisk, the most honored of Grandstand Football Greats, earned his reputation by attending nearly 100 Notre Dame games without once ever yelling, "We want a touchdown!"

## JASPER C. VAN FLICK
### Harvard '47

Van Flick was banned from attending Ivy League football contests after it was discovered that he'd actually raised his voice during a cheer at the 1946 Harvard—Princeton classic.

**END**

*This next article concerns itself with the art of...*

# CHANGING MEANINGS FOR FUN & PROFIT

It's a common practice among sly Broadway and Hollywood producers to pick out certain words from a panning newspaper review, substitute dots for the other words they ignore, and thereby cleverly turn a pan review into a rave review. For example, here's a review which blasts a new film. The producer of the movie underlines certain words . . .

# "The Mighty And The Sick"

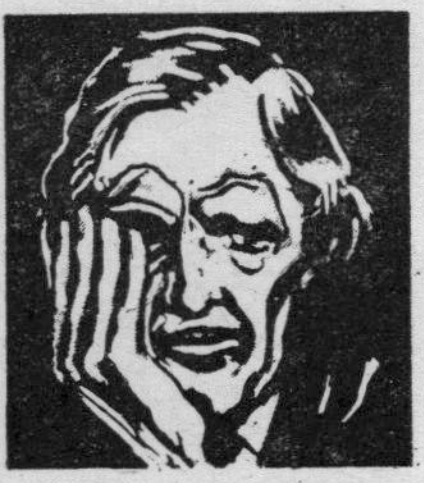

## *A Bitter Disappointment*

**BY BOSWELL CHOWDER**

*Copyright 1959, Alfred E. Neuman Syndicate*

Seldom does a film reviewer have an urge to smash a producer in the nose, and hit the director in the eye. But that's exactly how I felt after seeing "The Mighty and The Sick" at the Cameo last night. It was so deeply disappointing that I kept moving from one seat to another to keep from falling asleep.

Stone Sfortz gives a superb imitation of a spastic marionette as he stumbles through his performance. On screen, he is as expressive as a Mongoloid idiot, and if he accepts his salary check for this role, he is a bigger bandit than I thought he was.

Dolores Fingerhut was never so miscast. Frankly, Bernie the Wonder Horse looked far more appealing.

One thing is sure: they should fire Oscar Pivnick for writing some of the poorest material ever seen on film.

Under no circumstances should you see it! I'll say it again: under no circumstances should you see it! And again: under no circumstances should you see it! and again . . .

The producer then takes all the underlined words, separates them by dots, and combines them to form the following blurb which he uses to exploit the film in newspaper ads and on posters.

# THE MIGHTY AND THE SICK

"The Mighty and The Sick" . . . a . . . smash . . . hit . . . deeply . . . moving . . . Stone Sfortz gives a superb . . . performance . . . as . . . a . . . Mongoloid . . . bandit . . . Dolores Finger- hut was never . . . more . . . appealing . . . sure . . . fire . . . Oscar . . . material . . . see it . . . again . . . and again . . . and again . . .

# AND HERE IS HOW
# EMPLOY THIS TECHNIQUE

## WANTED BY THE F.B.I.

FBI 72210   FBI 72210

### CONSTANTIN SNURDLEY

Alias "Honest Connie", Alias "Reliable Snurd"
33 years old, 185 pounds, 5' 10"

## $15,000 REWARD!

Escaped a year ago from F.B.I. Man guarding him has never been seen since.

Permanently scarred by knife on upper right forearm.

Has habit of whistling tunes like "Temptation" and "It's A Sin to Tell a Lie" when casing banks.

Doesn't show mercy, will not hesitate to kill any time when on a job.

Recommend extreme caution when dealing with Snurdley.

To any person spotting him: he is a first class killer, always carries a machine gun, even when shop-lifting.

J. EDGAR HOOVER

To All Postmasters: I recommend that, for best results, this Wanted Notice be placed in a prominent place in all Post Offices.

ARTHUR SUMMERFIELD, Postmaster General

# OTHER PEOPLE MIGHT SUCCESSFULLY

 Constantin Snurdley, an escaped criminal, sees this circular in a Post Office. He mentally underlines some of the words . . .

And when Snurdley applies for a legitimate job, he's got two wonderful references . . .

## HARLEY'S MACHINE SHOP

### Application for Employment

NAME: *Constantin Snurdley*

SCHOOLING: *Dannemora*   DEGREE: *3rd.*

REFERENCES *Here's what J. Edgar Hoover, of Washington, D.C., said about me: "Constantin Snurdley ... honest ... reliable ... $15,000 ... a year ... man ... never ... scarred by ... Temptation ... and ... Sin ... Doesn't ... kill ... time ... on a ... job ... Recommend ... Snurdley to any ... first class ... machine ... shop ..." Arthur Summerfield, also of Washington, said this: "Recommend ... for ... prominent ... Post ..."*

Connem and Bullem, Advertising
733 West 42nd Street
New York, N.Y.

Gentlemen:
Please place a classified ad in the paper for me. You may use the in-
formation in this letter as a guide.
I have a dog I would like to sell. He is a big, ugly animal, with huge
ears, and he has been living in my home against my wishes for five
months. He's got 23 breeds in him, and we call him "Doberman" because
he facially resembles that member of Sgt. Bilko's platoon. He likes
to eat sulphur, and since he's been here, the house is matchless.
He's always falling down the cellar steps and rolling in the coal bin,
which gives him a black coat to go with his natural brown, white,
gray, green, red, and cerise one.
The police said they would fine me if I let him out, and I think he'd
be dangerous in a house with children. His sire was a champion
Chicken-Killer.
A friend of mine with the American Kennel Club registered surprise
when he saw this monster. He said the mutt was so hideous, he couldn't
believe it was real. Sometimes, I don't believe it myself. We've
innoculated the dog for every possible disease, but he gets them anyway. The only one he's missed so far has been the measles.
Please place an ad and get rid of him for me. Everything he's touched
in the house is broken.
Oh-oh! I've just noticed he's getting some red blotches now!

                                        Very truly yours,
                                        Marvin Skroog.

An advertising agency
receives this letter
and immediately under-
lines important words:

Next day this classi-
fied ad appears in
the pet section of
the local newspaper:

DOBERMAN . . . matchless . . .
coal . . . black . . . fine . . . with
children . . . sire . . . champion . . .
American Kennel Club registered
. . . innoculated . . . house . . .
broken . . . write BOX M-3 TIMES

# INDEPENDENT VETERINARY HOSPITAL
## Khartoum, Sudan
### MEDICAL BULLETIN #47

NOTICE TO OUR <u>TWO</u> CUSTODIANS, OUR <u>OUT OF</u> TOWN RESIDENT SURGEON, AND OUR <u>THREE</u> HORSE <u>DOCTORS</u>:

DO NOT SPIT, <u>SMOKE</u>, OR CARRY A LIGHTED PIPE OR CIGAR ON THESE PREMISES. THIS PRACTICE ENDANGERS THE HEALTH OF THE <u>CAMELS</u> AND OTHER ANIMALS IN THIS HOSPITAL.

VIOLATION OF THIS ORDER IS PUNISHABLE BY A FINE OF FIVE HUNDRED DOLLARS, A YEAR IN PRISON, OR BOTH.

The following bulletin is spotted by an employee of an American cigarette company while traveling abroad. He copies it down, underlines vital words, and sends it to N. Y.

A week later, during a network TV program, the following appears on the Teleprompter for the announcer to read to the country:

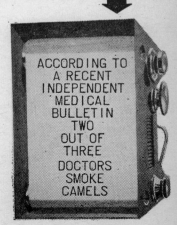

ACCORDING TO A RECENT INDEPENDENT MEDICAL BULLETIN TWO OUT OF THREE DOCTORS SMOKE CAMELS

Seymour Getzoff
6B1

P.S. 193
Brooklyn, N.Y.

My Vacation

My vacation this year was a very interesting one. I did not expect it to be so interesting. Uusually, I am against going to the mountains. But when my Mother and Father took me to the Cat-skills, I found the country to be very pleasant. I enjoyed the lake and everything. It was nice. We visited refreshment stands on the way for ice cream and sodas.

One day, my Father said, "Let us go to town while Seymour takes his afternoon nap. We will bring back a nice book for him." I had fun while they were gone.

That evening, they returned with "Up From Slavery" by Booker T. Washington. It was a very interesting book. I enjoyed it. I never knew Booker T. Washington was such a good student.

The next day, my Father and Mother took me to a movie in town. Of course, we had a good time. We saw the Marx Brothers. How I laughed.

I believe we would be better off next summer if we went to a smaller hotel, though. This place was so large that I lost my notebook. I think I left it under a Red Bench in the Lobby. I also lost my ruler somewhere.

My vacation was very interesting.

Seymour Getzoff.

During an election campaign, one nominee digging for dirt on his opponent comes across this composition written 25 years ago for a sixth year grammar school class.

And a week later, this crafty, unscrupulous nominee gives a hair-raising political speech:

I have in my hand a damaging piece of evidence. It is a document written and signed by my opponent in this election. Let me quote some excerpts from this shocking document: "I am against the country . . . and everything it . . . stands for . . . Let us . . . bring back . . . Slavery . . . Washington was . . . a . . . student . . . of . . . Marx . . . I believe we would be better off . . . under a Red . . . ruler . . ."

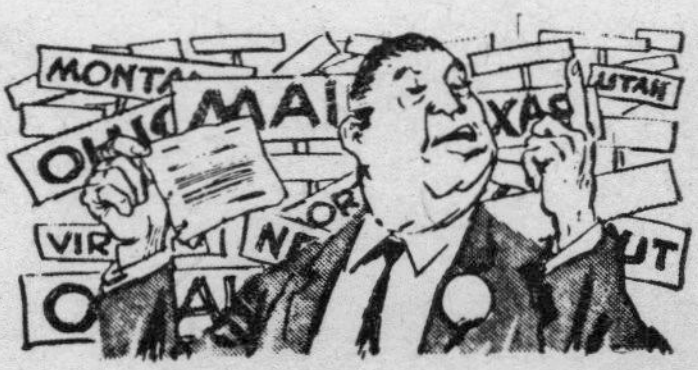
MONTA
UTAH
VIR
UT



END

And now, Don Martin tells us about the time he joined the Volunteer Fire Department, and was assigned to the life net brigade during...

# THE GREAT HOTEL FIRE

2

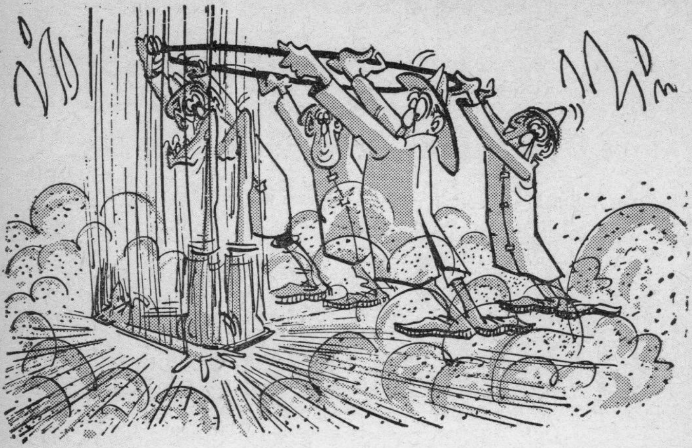

3

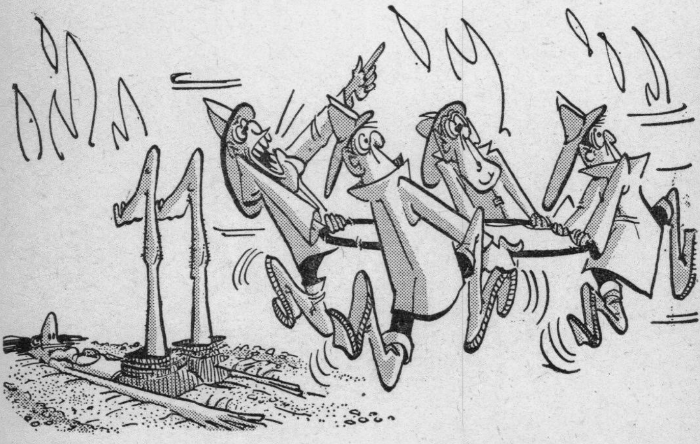

4

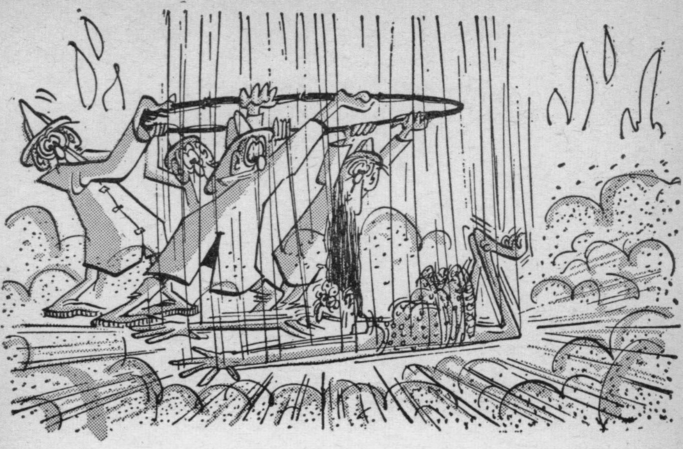

5

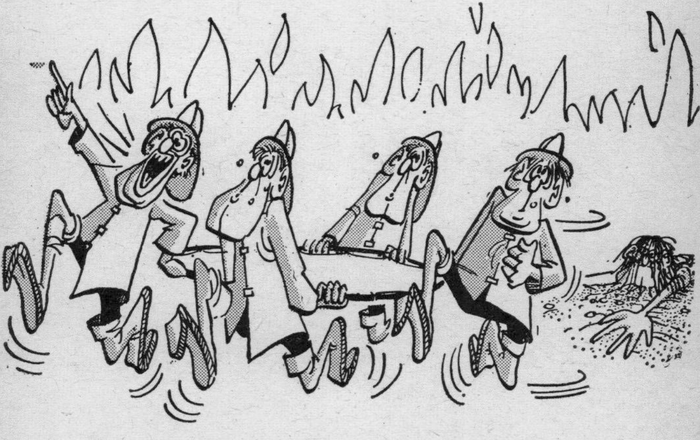

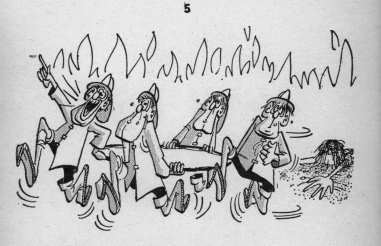

6

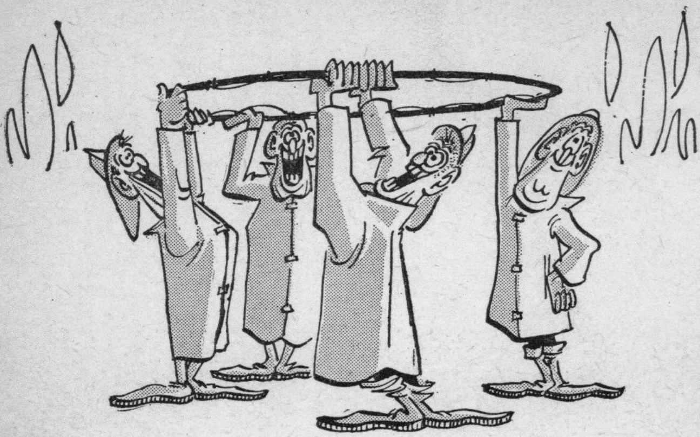

7

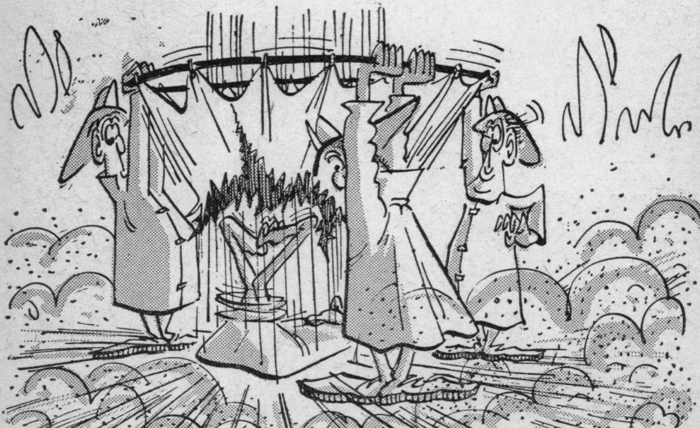
D. MARTIN

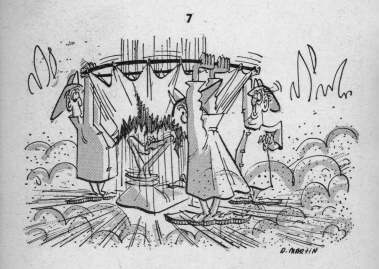

END

## ROCK 'N PAROLE DEPT.

Let's face it! Today, a high school isn't much different from a prison. Bells ring announcing different activities, there are guards in the halls, students gather in cliques to secretly plot how to escape by cutting classes, relatives come to visit (when cutters are caught), weapons in the form of crib notes are cleverly smuggled into exams, etc. The only difference we can see is: high schools have yearbooks, and prisons don't! We think it's only fair that the graduating inmates of prisons all over the country are entitled to the same permanent remembrance of the best years of their lives. For example:

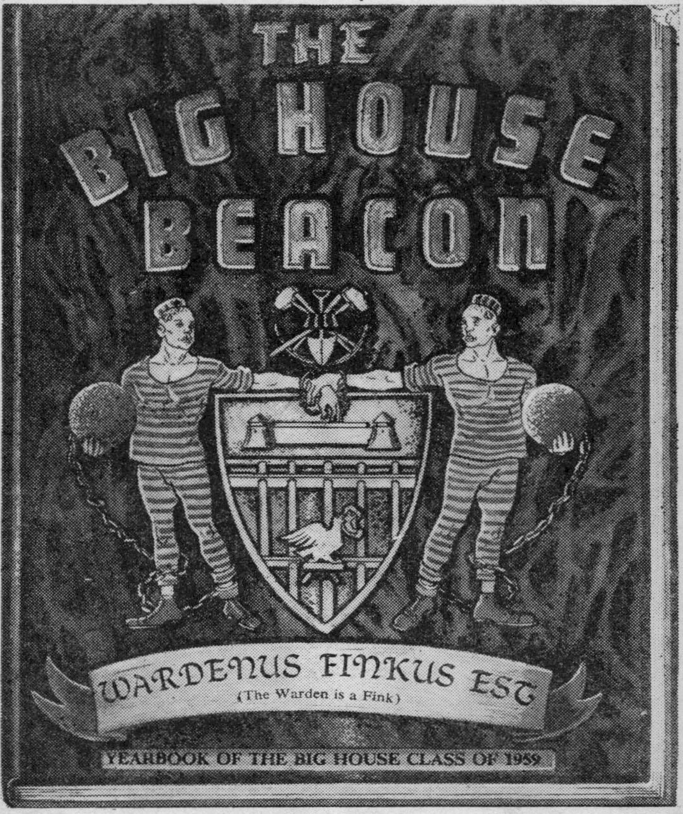
THE
BIG HOUSE
BEACON
WARDENUS FINKUS EST
(The Warden is a Fink)
YEARBOOK OF THE BIG HOUSE CLASS OF 1959

# BIG HOUSE
# HONOR GRADUATES

### Albanese, Rocky
#### 5-10 BURGLARY
##### Served 7

Solitary Confinement Section Monitor, Bar - Clanging and Guard-Baiting Club, Calendar Date Scratcher-Outer for Cell 34

A swell guy to all, a friend through and through,
Unless you're a guard, a fink or a screw.

### Carson, Arson
#### 10-12 EMBEZZLING
##### Served 4

Legal Loopholes and Appeals Club, Sheet-Knotting Society, Getting Word to the Outside Committee, Ducking - The - Searchlight Certificate.

Always light-hearted, smiling and gay,
Knowing he's got ten grand stashed away.

## Fagin, Seymour

**10-20 HIJACKING**

**Served 6 Months**

President of the Barton MacLane Fan Club, Side-of-the-Mouth Message-Passing Certificate, Captain of the Senior Stoolie-Beating Team, Laundry-Room Gun-Smuggling Award.

**Eyes of blue, a smile so wide,**
**He'll kill his mouthpiece**
**when he gets outside.**

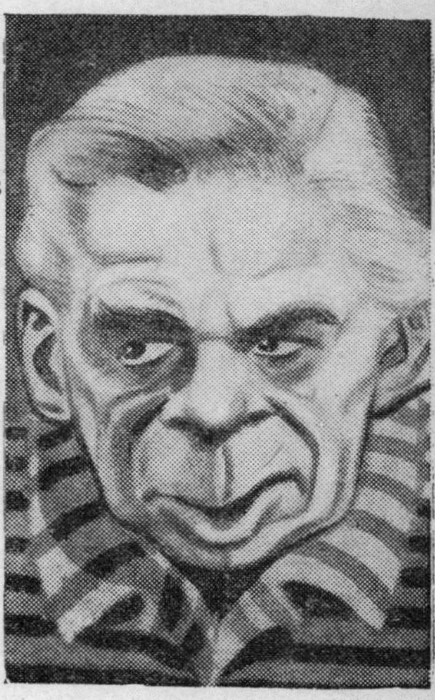

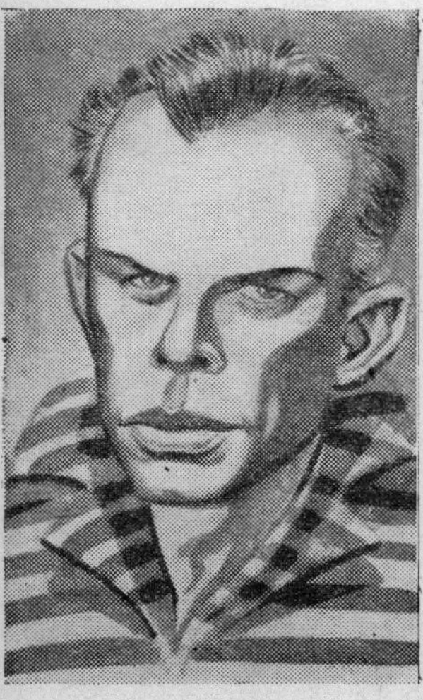

## Noonan, Burnside

**2-5 ASSAULT**

**Served 17**

Dining Hall Riot-Starting Squad, Death House Glee Club, Big Bull Manesi's Shakedown Committee, Note-Swallowing Honor Society.

**Bright and cheery, a mischievous elf,**
**In three pens he's made a**
**number for himself.**

## Throop, Trigger

### 15-20 MANSLAUGHTER
#### Served 11

Yard Rumor-Spreading Squad, Playboy Magazine Pin-Up Hanging Monitor, Prison Prom Social Director, Treasurer of the Jack La Rue Fan Club.

Smart and handsome, an emcee rare
For our prison TV show "Beat The Chair".

## Zinn, Zack

### 7-10 JAYWALKING
#### Served 15

Society Editor of Big House Bugle, Prison Break Hostage-Holding Monitor, Secretary of the Nat Pendleton Fan Club.

Roses are red, violets are blue, Mustard is hot, his car was too.

# BIG HOUSE SQUADS AND ORGANIZATIONS

## THE SENIOR MACHINE SHOP CREW

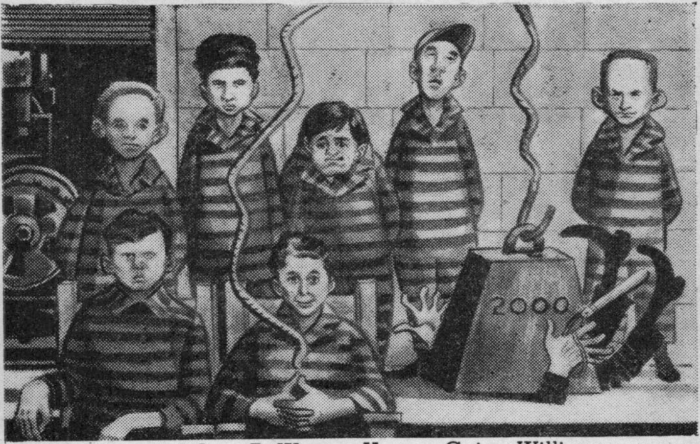
2000

*Standing:* L. to R. Warren Hymer, Guinn Williams, Leo Gorcey, Huntz Hall, Louis Fink (a guard) and Edward Brophy. *Seated:* Harold Huber, Billy Halop *Dropping:* One-Ton Weight

## THE SENIOR STOOLIE SQUAD

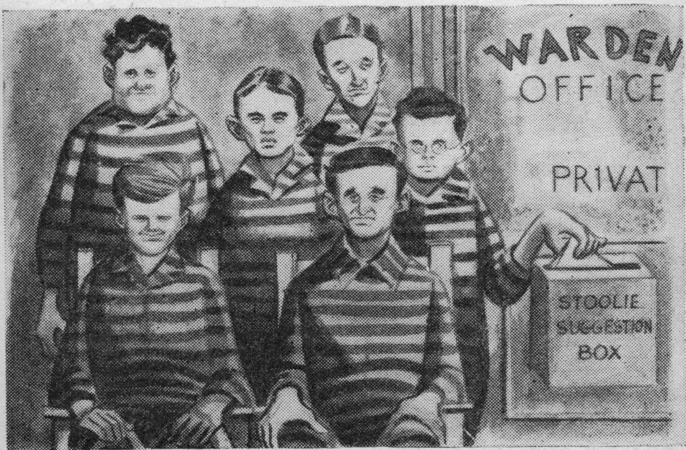
WARDEN
OFFICE
PR1VAT
STOOLIE
SUGGESTION
BOX

L. to R. the late Chick McGooley, the late Hank Borelli, the late Ike Yurks, the late Monty McGee, the late Irv Dillinger, the late Lait Show.

# OUTSTANDING
# BIG HOUSE GRADUATES

## BEST DRESSED

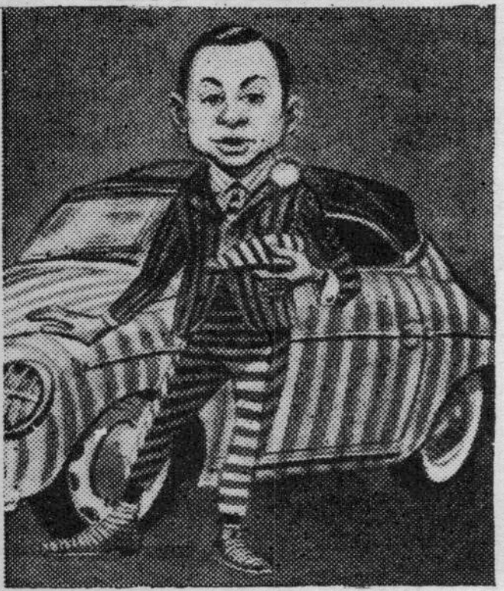

WARREN BIGGLEBY

## MOST POPULAR

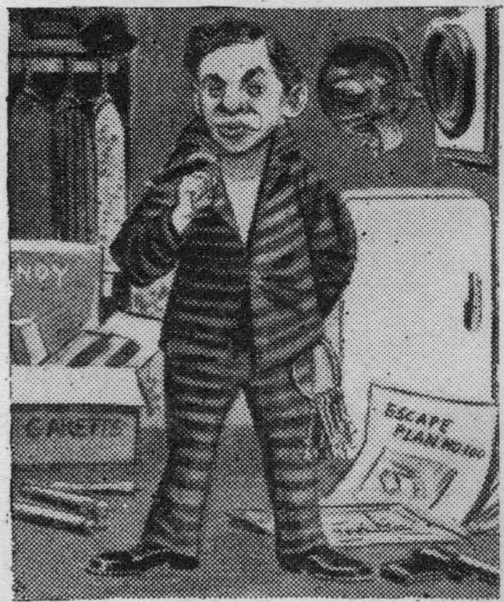
ESCAPE
PLAN

MURRAY FINSTER

## COMEDIAN

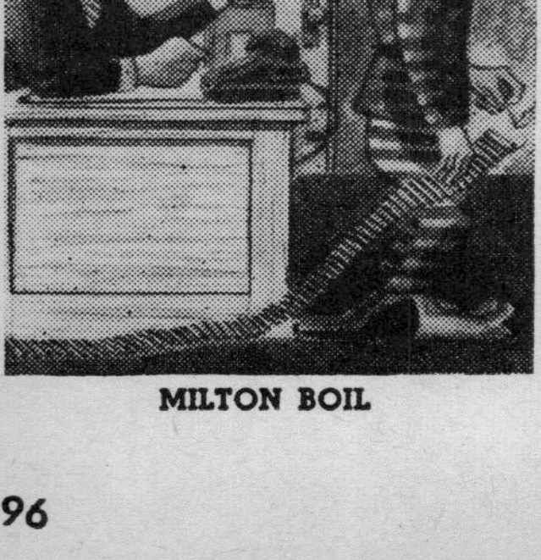

MILTON BOIL

## MOST LIKELY TO SUCCEED

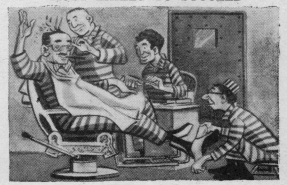

BORIS WILLEWSKI

## LEAST LIKELY TO SUCCEED

MACHINE GUN GERTZ

# CANDID SHOTS OF THE CLASS OF '59

THE BOYS IN SOLITARY
AT NOON

THE BOYS IN SOLITARY
AT MIDNIGHT

SENIORS PLAYING
"CATCH THE STOOLIE"

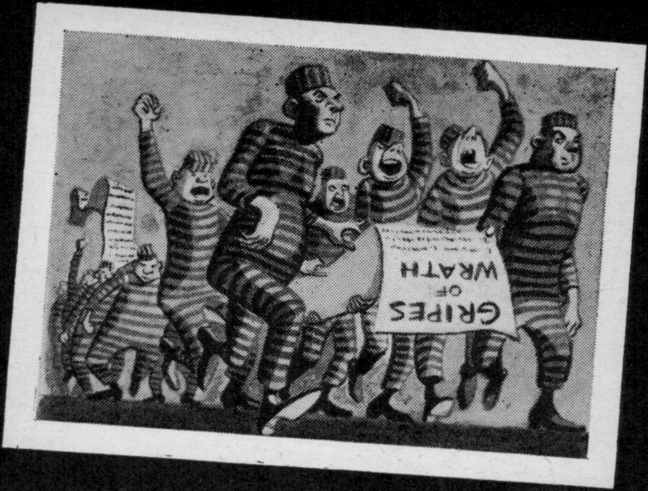
GRIPES
OF
WRATH

PRISON COMMITTEE GOING TO WARDEN'S OFFICE WITH A LIST OF GRIEVANCES

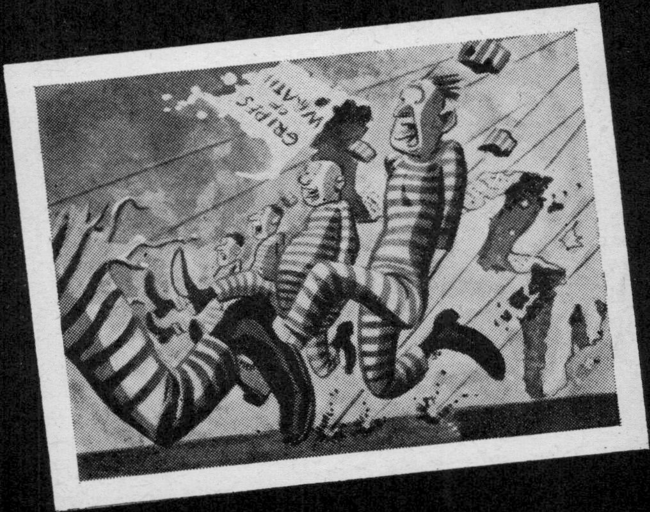

PRISON COMMITTEE RETURNING FROM WARDEN'S OFFICE WITH A LIST OF GRIEVANCES

BIG HOUSE ACROBATIC TEAM PRACTICING
FOR ATHLETIC MEET WITH SING SING

SENIORS PLAYING "BRIBE THE GUARD"
BEHIND THE PRISON LIBRARY

# BIG HOUSE SONGS AND CHEERS

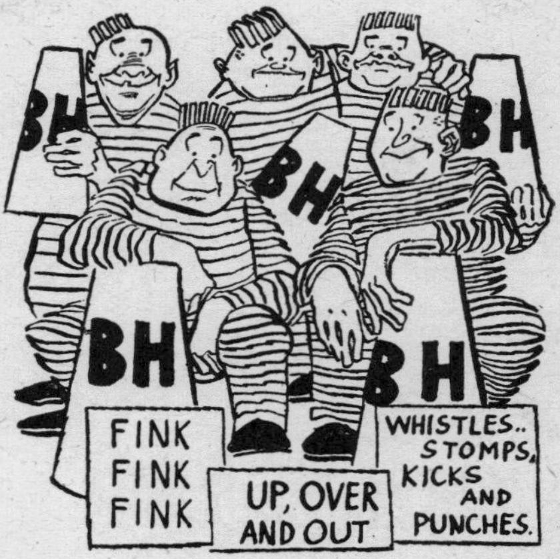
BH
BH
BH
BH
BH
FINK
FINK
FINK
UP, OVER
AND OUT
WHISTLES..
STOMPS,
KICKS
AND
PUNCHES.

## ALMA MATER

Alma Mater, Alma Mater,
To your praise our voices ring ring.
San Quentin, Alcatraz can't touch you,
And we prefer you to Sing Sing.
We love your ivy-covered cell blocks,
The peace your Solitary gives,
We walk your yard in autumn sunsets
Making mess spoons into shivs.
Alma Mater, Alma Mater,
Unto you we raise a cup,
Of all the pens throughout the nation,
Yours is the river we want to go up
    Up, up, up . . .
Yours is the river we want to go up.

## THE DINING HALL CHANT

*(To be sung while clanging silverware on the dining hall tables. For proper rhythm, see any of the last 17 Barton MacLane pictures)*

Ya ya  ya ya
Ya ya  ya ya
Ya ya  ya ya
Ya ya  ya ya  ya ya  ya ya
Ya ya  ya ya  ya ya  ya ya
Ya ya  ya ya  ya ya  ya ya  ya ya
Ya ya  ya ya  ya ya  ya ya  ya ya
Ya ya  ya ya  ya ya  ya ya  ya ya  ya ya
Baby!

## GO CHEER

Come on, Big House, on the ball!
Let's not stumble, let's not fall!
Grab a hostage, big or small!
Blow a hole in the west wall!
Then, go, team
Go, team
GO! GO! GO!

## SPELL-IT-OUT CHEER

With a "B" and an "I" and a double "G"
And an "H" and an "O" and a "W-S-E"
**BIGG HOWSE!!!**
*(Wait, that's not right, fellas!)*
With a "B" and an "I" and then a "J"
And an "H" and an "O" and an "O-S-E"
**BIJ HOOSE???**
*(Let's try it again, huh gang)*
With a "B" and an "I" and then a "K"
And an "H" and an "A" and . . .
*(Aw, the heck with it!)*
**YEY, TEAM!!!**

# A MESSAGE FROM OUR WARDEN

## TO THE BIG HOUSE GRADUATING CLASS OF 1959

It has been our job here at Big House to teach you right from wrong. We have attempted to impress you with the words of Buggus Bunnius, the famous Latin scholar, who said: "*Stratus winnus; lorbrakus losus; paisus stratus shutus!*" Which means: "Straight-shooters always win, law-breakers always lose, so it pays to shoot straight!"

At last you are ready to go out into the world. As is customary, I now give you each a suit of clothes and $10. You are now good, fine, honest men. And now, I must say good-bye. I must re-deposit the rest of this $10,000 dollars I drew from the vault, and . . . hmmmm . . .

I could have sworn I had the money in my pocket a few minutes ago . . .

Your Warden
OTTO WILTSHIRE

# A MESSAGE FROM OUR ADMISSIONS OFFICER

## TO THE BIG HOUSE GRADUATING CLASS OF 1959

You are now the Big House Graduating Class of 1964, if you don't try anything else like you just pulled on the Warden. Please remove all your clothing, and leave your valuables at the desk . . .

Your Admissions Officer
ALVIN FLUT

**END**

DEPT.

THIS ARTICLE CONCERNS ITSELF WITH THE CRAZE
BECAUSE IT APPEALS TO MAN'S NATURAL DESIRE

# PAIN

# BY THE

BEFORE "PAINTING BY THE NUMBERS,"

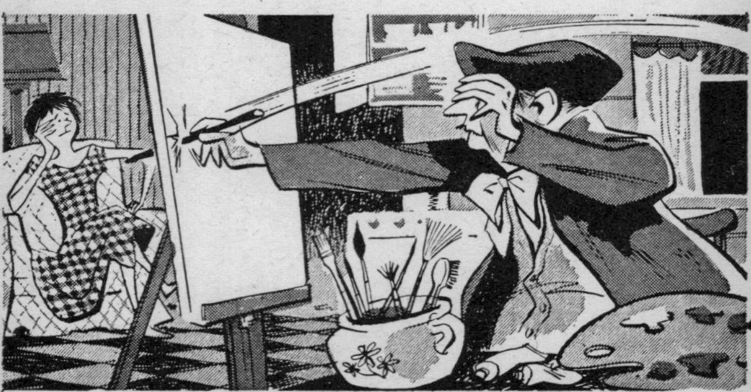

Would-be artist doesn't know where to start, so he guesses.

THAT HAS ZOOMED IN POPULARITY MAINLY
TO DO AS LITTLE THINKING AS POSSIBLE

# TING

# NUMBERS

THERE WAS ROOM FOR ERROR

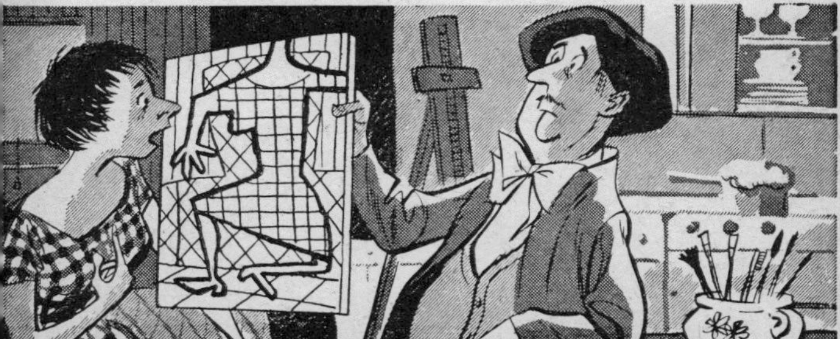

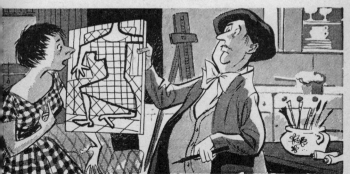

Results: He winds up with poor outline drawing and layout.

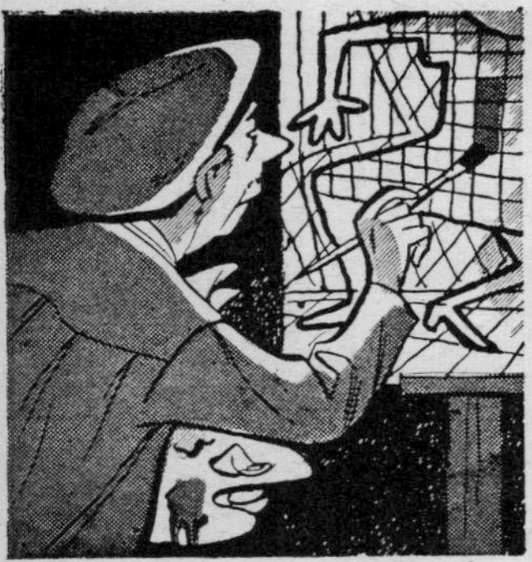

Next, he starts coloring in outline drawing with paints.

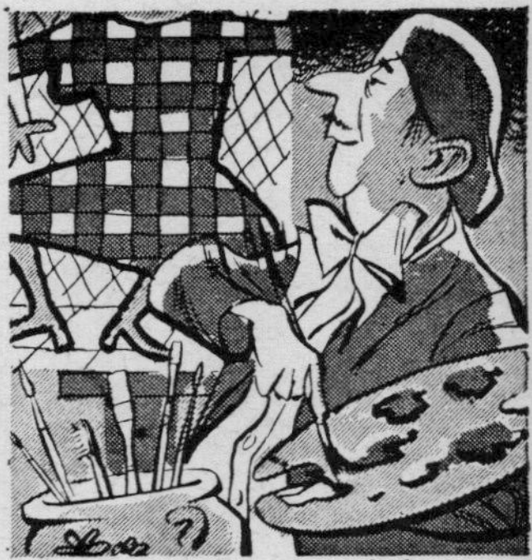

Paints in foreground design with nice attractive colors.

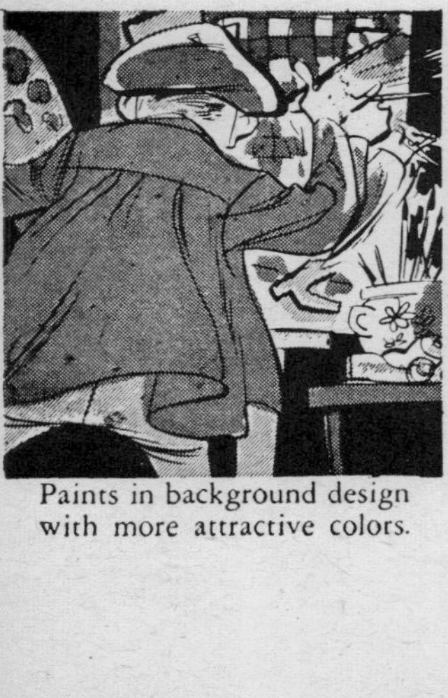

Paints in background design with more attractive colors.

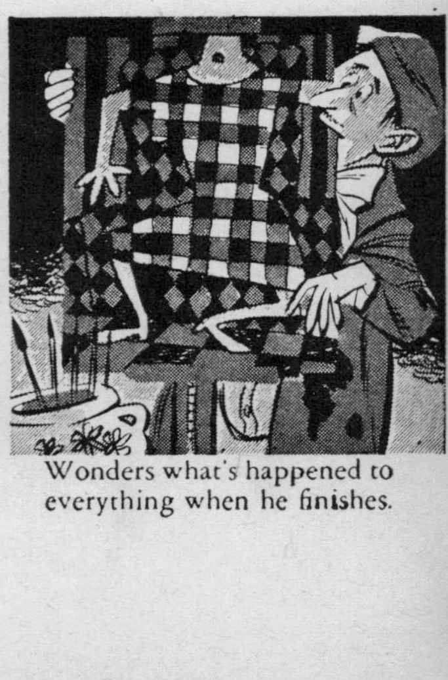

Wonders what's happened to everything when he finishes.

# WITH "PAINTING BY THE NUMBERS," THERE IS NO ROOM FOR ERROR

Would-be artist is supplied with a "professional" outline drawing and layout. All he has to do is read the numbers,

take tubes of paint with corresponding numbers, and fill in marked areas. Results is a perfect picture every time.

# MAD PROPOSES TO ELIMINATE
# APPLYING THIS MARVELOUS

## SURGERY BY THE NUMBERS

Takes the guesswork away, and guarantees

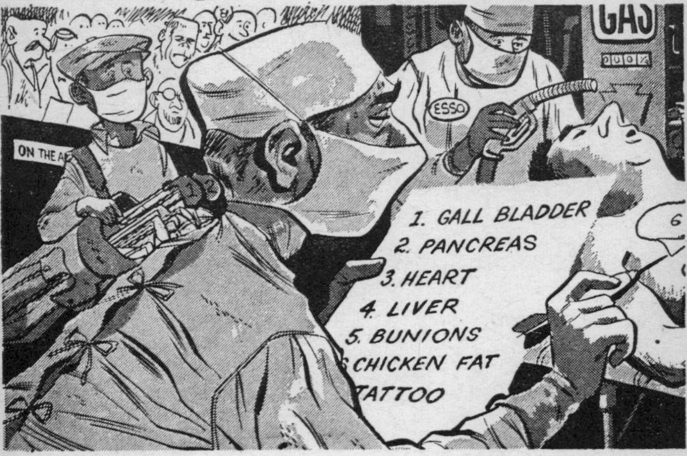
GAS
ESSO
ON THE A
1. GALL BLADDER
2. PANCREAS
3. HEART
4. LIVER
5. BUNIONS
CHICKEN FAT
TATTOO

## COOKING AND BAKING BY

Making pizza pie becomes a snap with

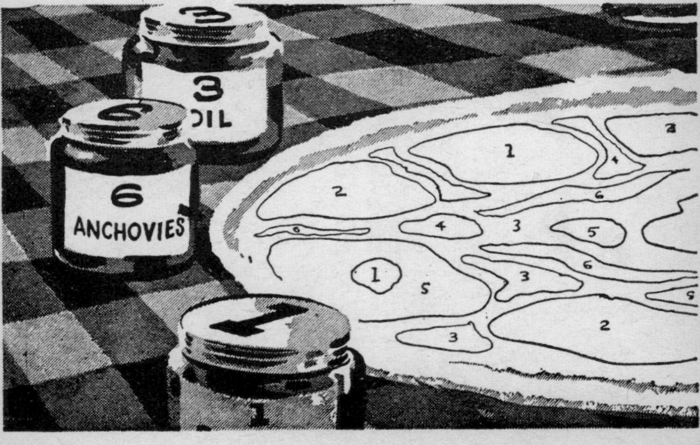
3
OIL
6
ANCHOVIES

# THINKING ENTIRELY BY METHOD TO OTHER FIELDS

a perfect operation every time.

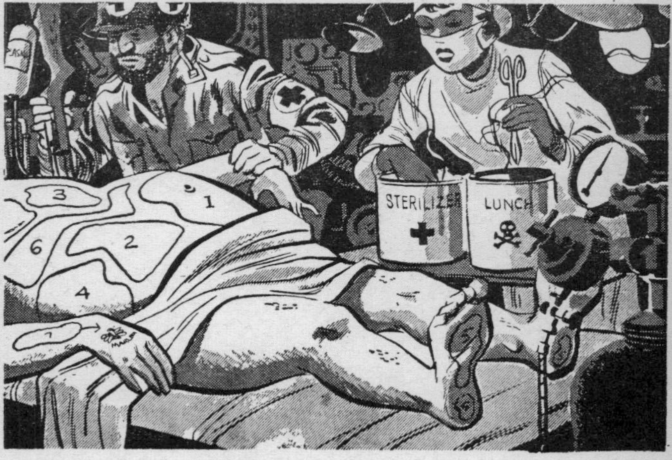
STERILIZER
LUNCH

## THE NUMBERS

numbered areas marked off on crust.

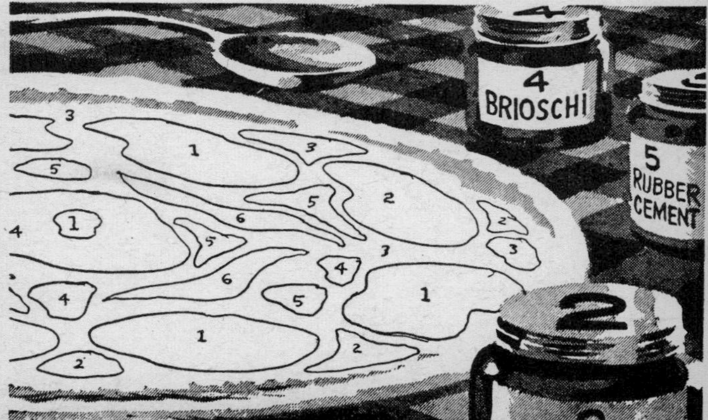
4
4
BRIOSCHI
5
RUBBER
CEMENT
2
2

## HOMEMAKING BY THE

No chance to make social blunders with

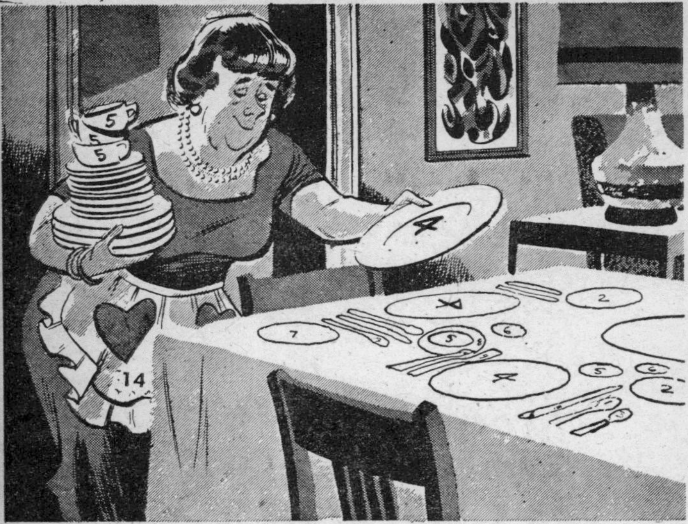

5
5
5
4
14
7
2
5
6
4
2


## CREATIVE WRITING BY THE

Pasting numbered words in corresponding

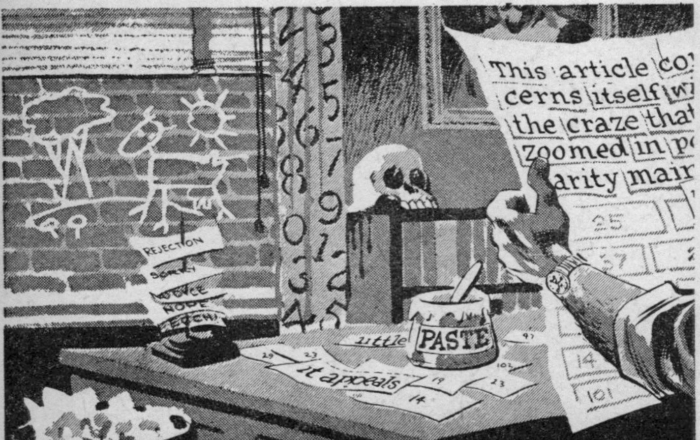

This article co
cerns itself wi
the craze that
zoomed in p
arity mai
REJECTION
little
PASTE
it appeals

**NUMBERS**

numbered tablecloth and tableware.

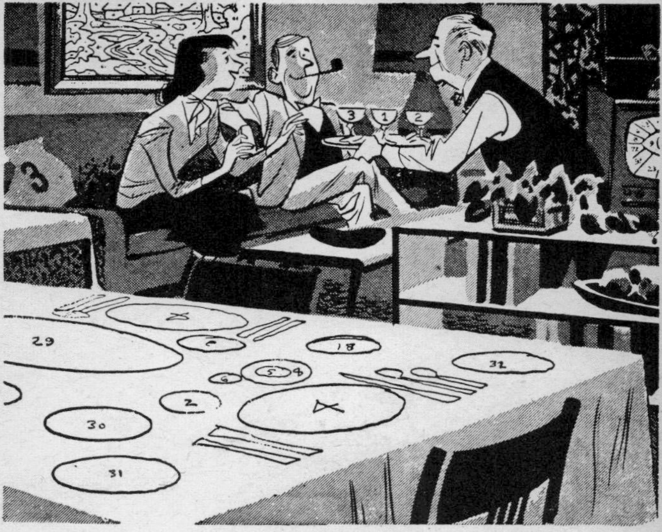

**NUMBERS**

spaces makes anybody a novelist.

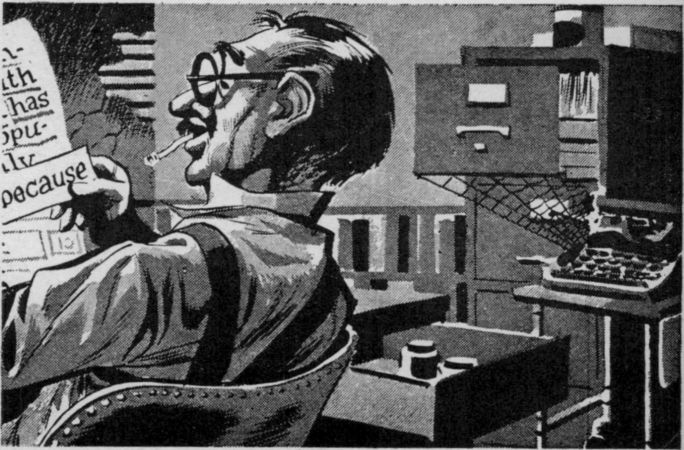

# BOXING BY THE NUMBERS

Best areas for drawing blood and inflicting

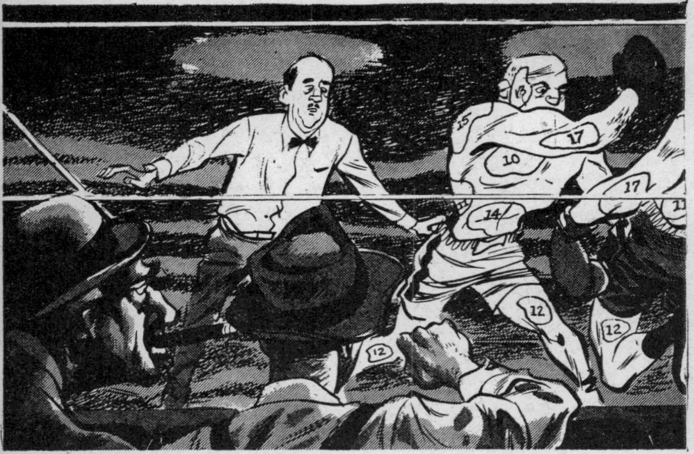

15
17
10
17
14
12
12
12


# WRESTLING BY THE NUMBERS

Progress of match is planned and numbered,

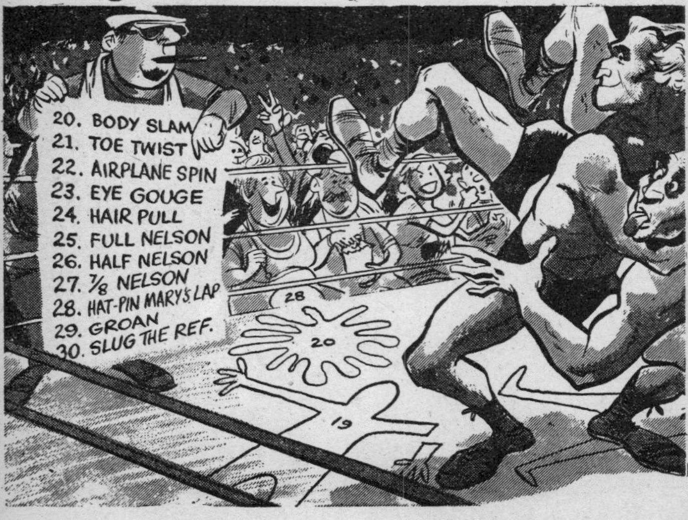

20. BODY SLAM
21. TOE TWIST
22. AIRPLANE SPIN
23. EYE GOUGE
24. HAIR PULL
25. FULL NELSON
26. HALF NELSON
27. 7/8 NELSON
28. HAT-PIN MARY'S LAP
29. GROAN
30. SLUG THE REF.
28
20
19

punishment are clearly marked.

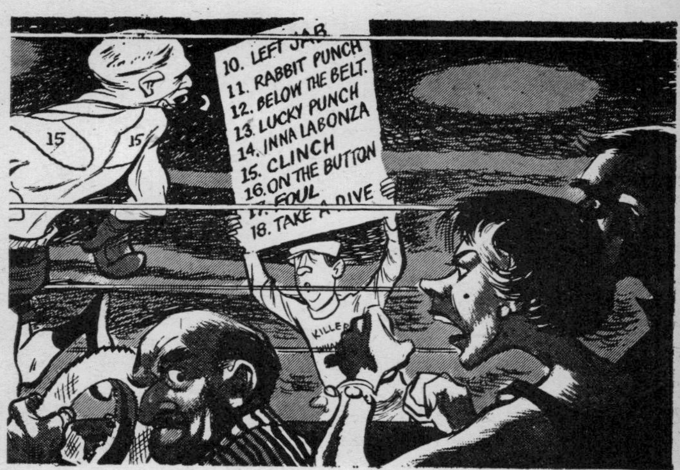
10. LEFT JAB
11. RABBIT PUNCH
12. BELOW THE BELT.
13. LUCKY PUNCH
14. INNA LABONZA
15. CLINCH
16. ON THE BUTTON
17. FOUL
18. TAKE A DIVE
KILLER

eliminating memorized scripts.

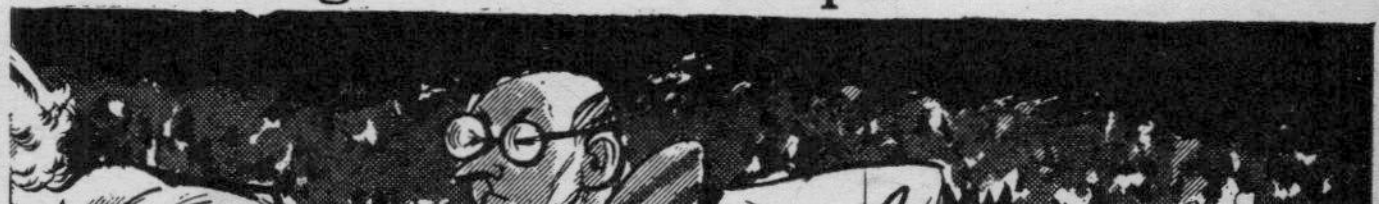
29
25.
21
Clarke

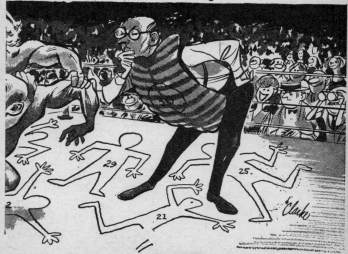

END

With about 50% of the population owning their own homes (in partnership with some banks), and with the cost of labor and materials sky high, the "home repair" problem has become a gigantic one. The tendency these days is to "do it yourself and save!" So we prepared the following article to help the situation. Mainly, you may not want to try it once you read...

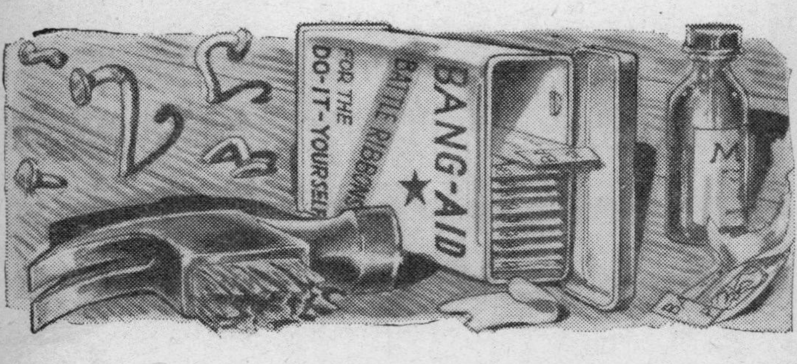
BANG-AID
BATTLE RIBBONS
FOR THE DO-IT-YOURSELF

# MAD's HELPFUL HOUSEHOLD REPAIR HINTS

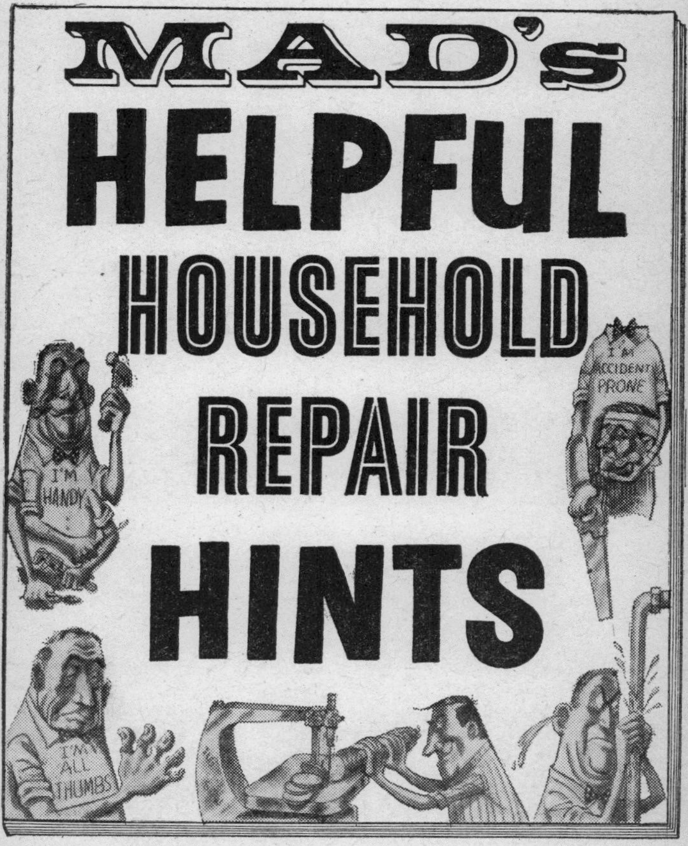
I'M HANDY
I AM ACCIDENT PRONE
I'M ALL THUMBS

# HOW TO FASTEN OBJECTS TO WALLS
## (WITHOUT CRACKING THE PLASTER)

To fasten object to wall without cracking plaster, place adhesive or cellophane tape over spot where nail is to go.

Drive nail through adhesive or cellophane tape. Note how tape prevents plaster from cracking directly beneath it.

# HOW TO CLEAR CLOGGED SINK DRAIN

If chemicals, snake, or the plumber's friend fails to unclog sink drain, trouble is usually in the sink trap.

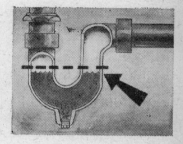

Clever sink trap works on principle that water seeks its own level, preventing odors from entering kitchen.

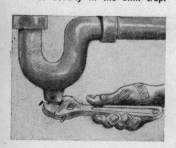

However, "U" shape tends to collect dirt, which blocks drainage. Use a wrench to remove plug at base of trap.

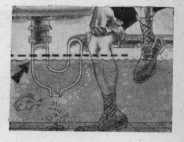

Dirt will be released. Also odors. Also plenty of water, and you'll see clearly how water seeks its own level.

# HOW TO REPAIR A DEFECTIVE LAMP

(1) An ordinary lamp socket is easily removed from its shell by depressing side of cap gently, and pulling up.

(2) Check for loose wires. If none, socket is probably defective. Remove it, and replace with a new socket.

(3) If lamp still does not work, the wire is probably defective. Remove it, and replace it with a new wire.

(4) If lamp still does not work, check if bulb's burnt out. That's usually what's wrong in the first place!

## HOW TO CLEAN A BLOCKED CHIMNEY

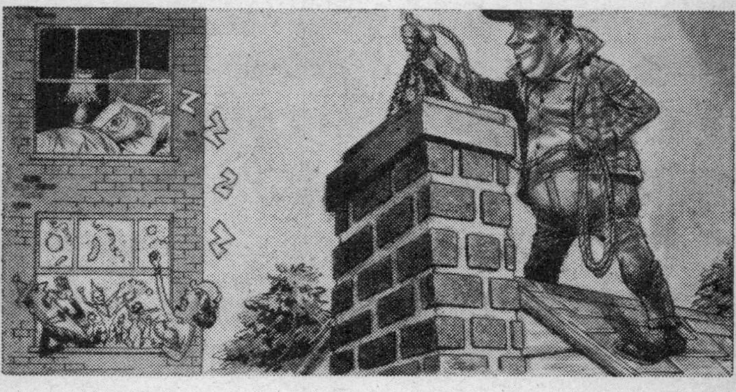

Tie weighted bag or tire chains to end of rope and lower into chimney. Shake the rope gently, hauling up and down.

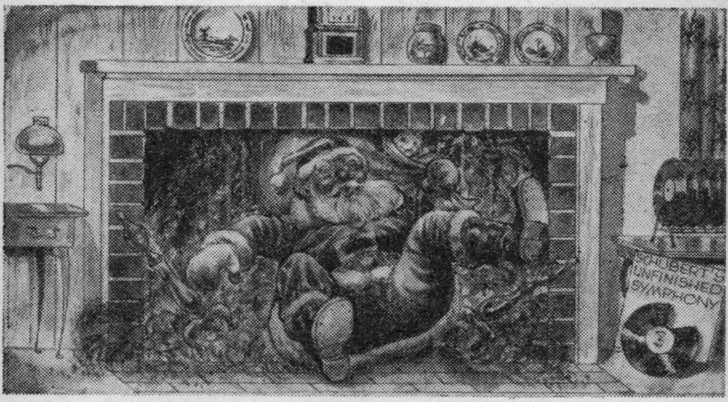
UNFINISHED
SYMPHONY

This will effectively loosen dirt, soot, and those other obstructions that may have been blocking up your chimney.

# HOW TO ELIMINATE A SQUEAKY FLOOR

Locate squeaky area and drive wedges between floor joists and all loose boards.

Drive finishing nails into 2 x 4 below, through squeaking boards, at sharp angle.

Nail length of 2 x 4 firmly against underside of floor boards in the squeaky area.

Squeaking will stop because all that pounding frightens off mice living under floor.

# HOW TO LOCATE A STUD BEHIND A WALL

To locate a wall stud, pad head of hammer with cloth.

Begin tapping along a wall, listening closely to sound.

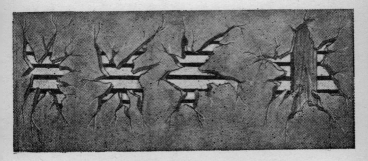

Spaces between studs emit hollow booming sound. When you hear dull muffled sound, you've finally located the stud.

# HOW TO REPAIR A DRAWER THAT WON'T SLIDE OPEN EASILY

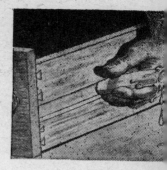

A stubborn sticking drawer may need sanding. If this does not cure trouble, all joints should be re-glued.

If drawer still sticks, see if bottom has slipped from grooves. Replace, and rub paraffin on sliding parts.

If drawer still won't slide open easily, try throwing out all the extra clothes and junk you've gathered in it over the years. You'll see how smoothly it'll work after that!

# HOW TO RELEASE A STICKING DOOR

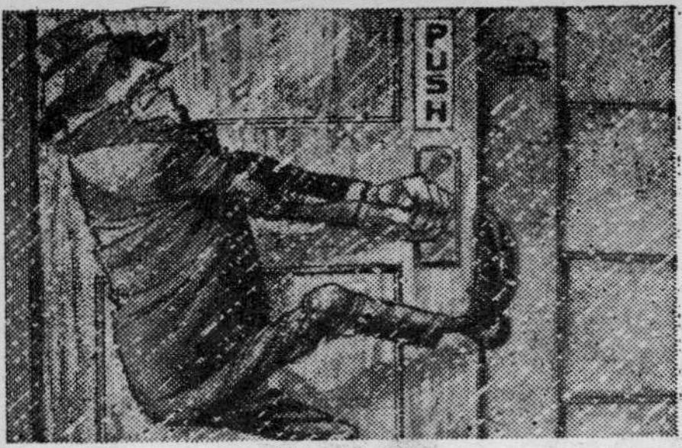
PUSH

If prolonged periods of rain or damp weather cause a door to stick so bad it can't be opened, here's what to do:

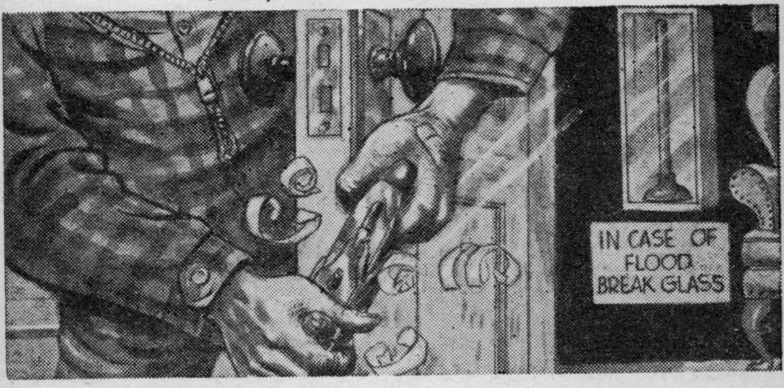
IN CASE OF FLOOD BREAK GLASS

Wedge door in open position and use a plane to shave down excess wood. Make sure you shave enough to release door.

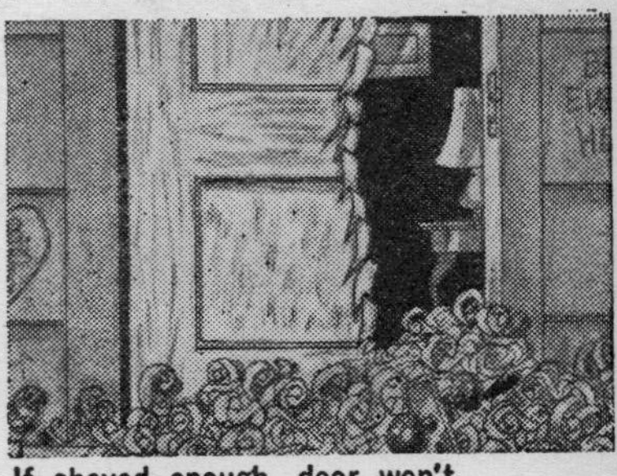

If shaved enough, door won't stick any more. If shaved too much, door won't even have to be opened any more.

# HOW TO REPAIR A LEAKY FAUCET

(1) Loosen and unscrew nut located under faucet handle.

(2) Remove faucet assembly by turning counterclockwise.

(3) Take out worn washer by removing screw securing it.

(4) Replace old washer with new one. Replace old screw.

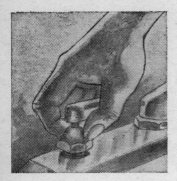

(5) Replace faucet assembly by turning unit clockwise.

(6) Rescrew and tighten nut located under faucet handle.

HALVAH
halvah
David Berg

Oh, yes! We forgot to tell you! . . . . Make sure that you shut off the water first, before you start fooling around!

END

# Scenes We'd Like to See

Driving The Golden Spike

1

PROMONTORY
POINT
2 MILES

2

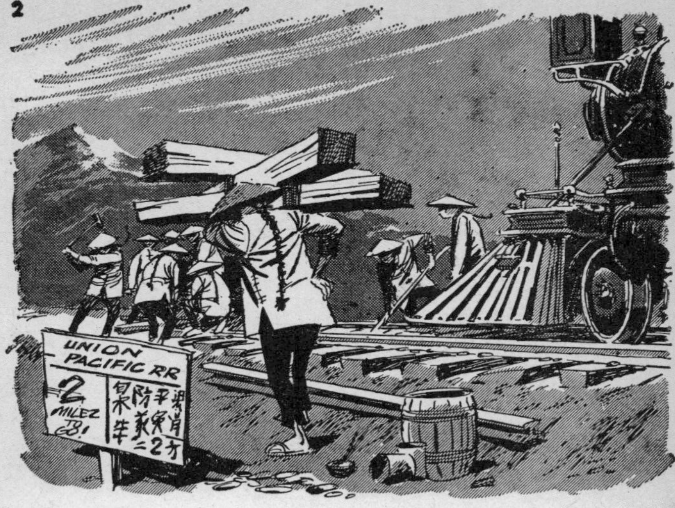
UNION
PACIFIC RR
2
MILEZ
TO GO!

3

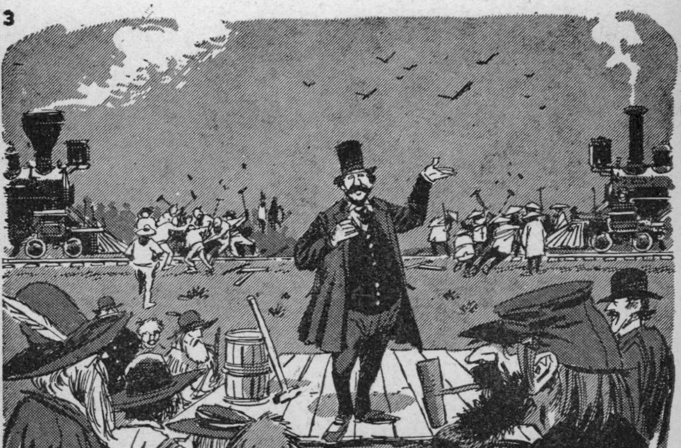

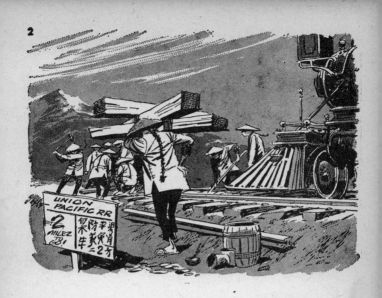

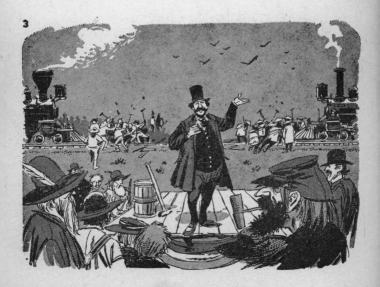

4

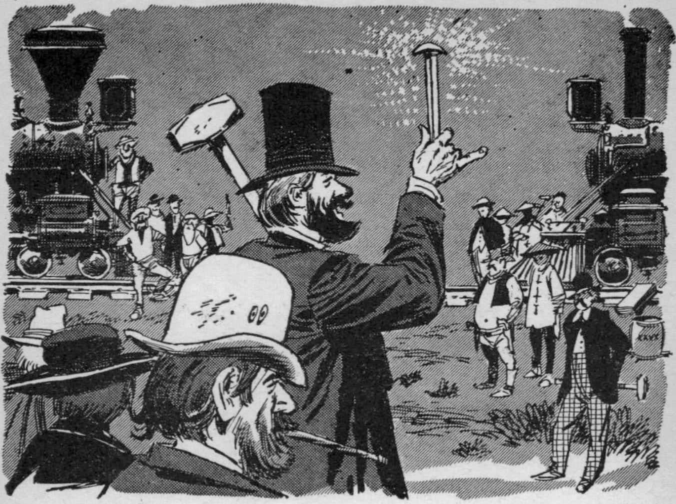

5

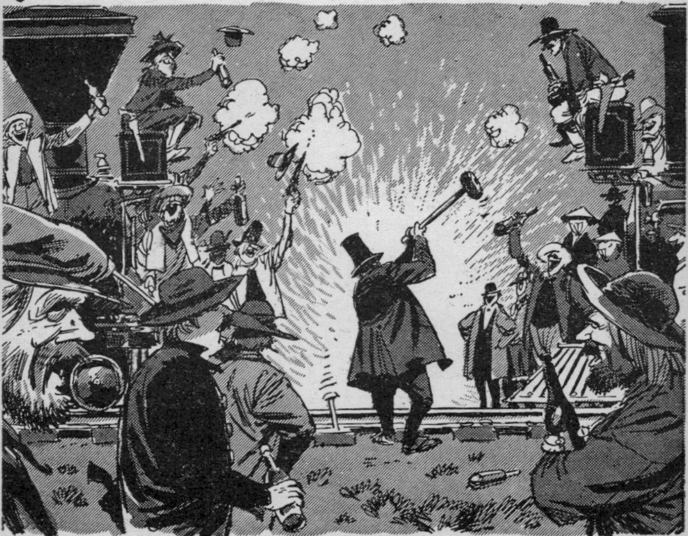

**E N D**

VERSE OF THE PEOPLE DEPT.

Some time ago (MAD #43), we dedicated our pages to some brilliant, but unknown, new American poets, in an effort to help these talented young writers get what they deserved. Since then, we have found several more who deserve the same thing. So here's

# THE MAD TREASURY OF UNKNOWN POETRY VOLUME II

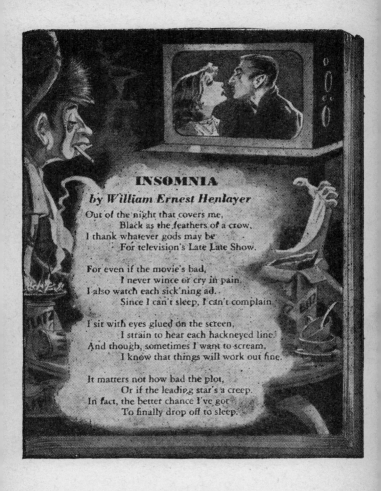

# INSOMNIA

## by William Ernest Henlayer

Out of the night that covers me,
    Black as the feathers of a crow,
I thank whatever gods may be
    For television's Late Late Show.

For even if the movie's bad,
    I never wince or cry in pain.
I also watch each sick'ning ad.
    Since I can't sleep, I can't complain.

I sit with eyes glued on the screen,
    I strain to hear each hackneyed line.
And though, sometimes I want to scream,
    I know that things will work out fine.

It matters not how bad the plot,
    Or if the leading star's a creep.
In fact, the better chance I've got
    To finally drop off to sleep.

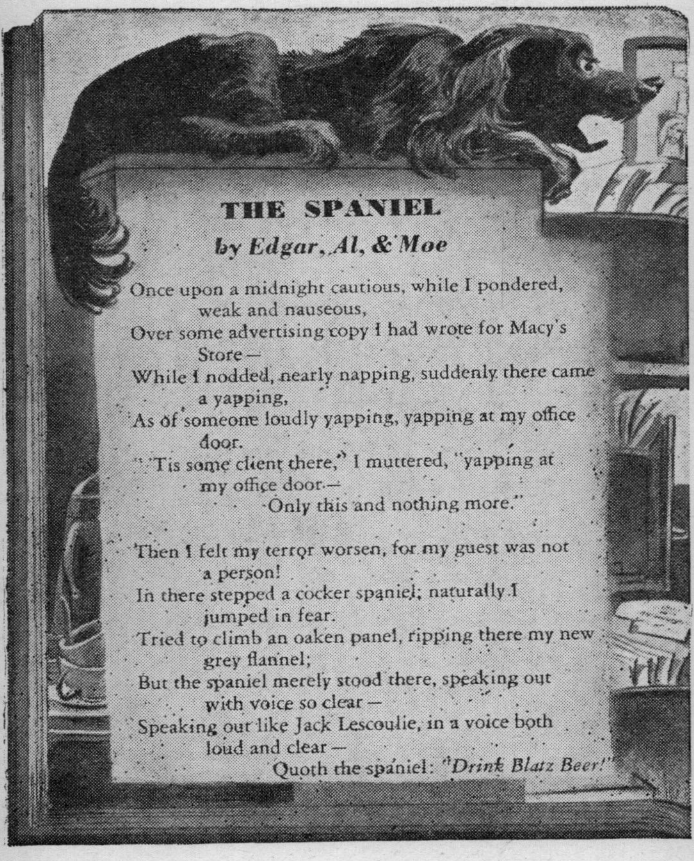

## THE SPANIEL

***by Edgar, Al, & Moe***

Once upon a midnight cautious, while I pondered,
weak and nauseous,
Over some advertising copy I had wrote for Macy's
Store —
While I nodded, nearly napping, suddenly there came
a yapping,
As of someone loudly yapping, yapping at my office
door.
"'Tis some client there," I muttered, "yapping at
my office door —
Only this and nothing more."

Then I felt my terror worsen, for my guest was not
a person!
In there stepped a cocker spaniel; naturally I
jumped in fear.
Tried to climb an oaken panel, ripping there my new
grey flannel;
But the spaniel merely stood there, speaking out
with voice so clear —
Speaking out like Jack Lescoulie, in a voice both
loud and clear —
Quoth the spaniel: *"Drink Blatz Beer!"*

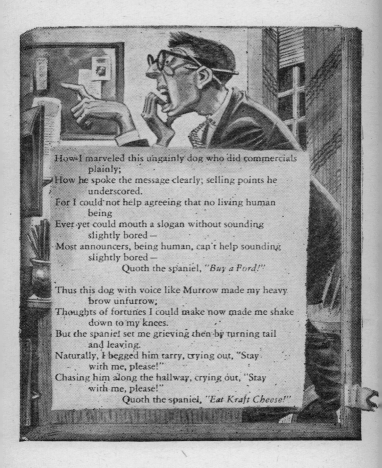

How I marveled this ungainly dog who did commercials
    plainly;
How he spoke the message clearly; selling points he
    underscored.
For I could not help agreeing that no living human
    being
Ever yet could mouth a slogan without sounding
    slightly bored —
Most announcers, being human, can't help sounding
    slightly bored —
        Quoth the spaniel, *"Buy a Ford!"*

Thus this dog with voice like Murrow made my heavy
    brow unfurrow;
Thoughts of fortunes I could make now made me shake
    down to my knees.
But the spaniel set me grieving then by turning tail
    and leaving.
Naturally, I begged him tarry, trying out, "Stay
    with me, please!"
Chasing him along the hallway, crying out, "Stay
    with me, please!"
        Quoth the spaniel, *"Eat Kraft Cheese!"*

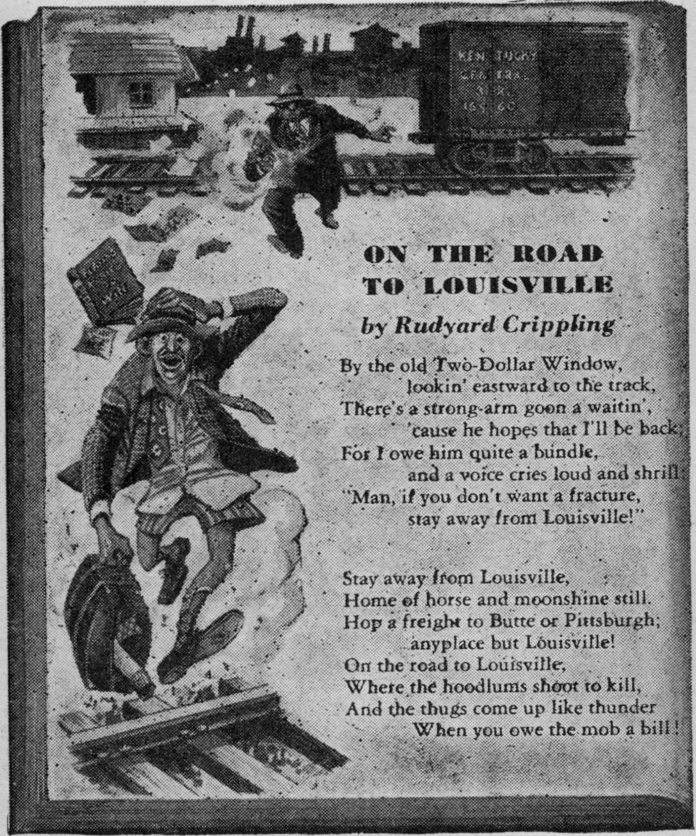

## ON THE ROAD TO LOUISVILLE

*by Rudyard Crippling*

By the old Two-Dollar Window,
lookin' eastward to the track,
There's a strong-arm goon a waitin',
'cause he hopes that I'll be back;
For I owe him quite a bundle,
and a voice cries loud and shrill:
"Man, if you don't want a fracture,
stay away from Louisville!"

Stay away from Louisville,
Home of horse and moonshine still.
Hop a freight to Butte or Pittsburgh;
anyplace but Louisville!
On the road to Louisville,
Where the hoodlums shoot to kill,
And the thugs come up like thunder
When you owe the mob a bill!

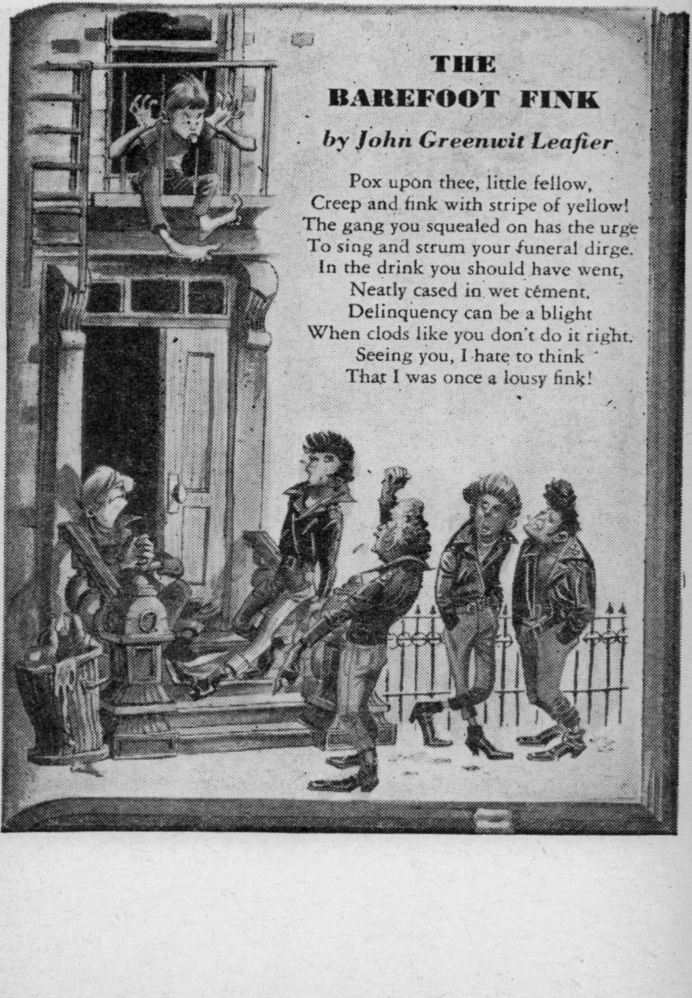

# THE BAREFOOT FINK

*by John Greenwit Leafier*

Pox upon thee, little fellow,
Creep and fink with stripe of yellow!
The gang you squealed on has the urge
To sing and strum your funeral dirge.
In the drink you should have went,
Neatly cased in wet cément.
Delinquency can be a blight
When clods like you don't do it right.
Seeing you, I hate to think
That I was once a lousy fink!

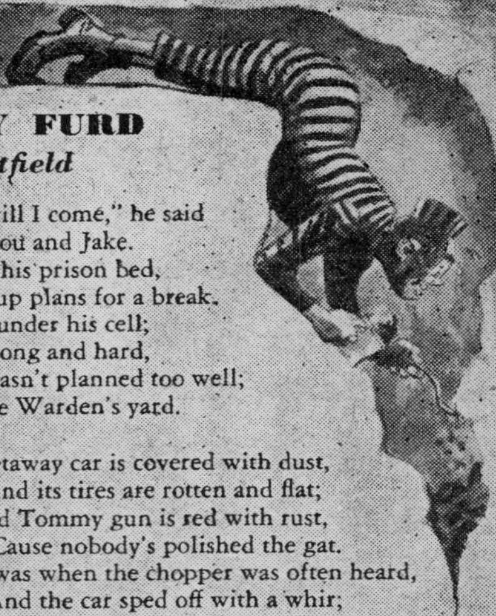

# KILLER BOY FURD

*by Eugene Outfield*

"Keep the gat and car till I come," he said
To his partners, Lou and Jake.
Then he toddled off to his prison bed,
And he dreamed up plans for a break.
He dug a tunnel from under his cell;
He worked on it long and hard,
But the route he dug wasn't planned too well;
He came up in the Warden's yard.

The getaway car is covered with dust,
And its tires are rotten and flat;
The old Tommy gun is red with rust,
'Cause nobody's polished the gat.
Time was when the chopper was often heard,
And the car sped off with a whir;
Then the cops came around for Killer Boy Furd
And put him away in stir.

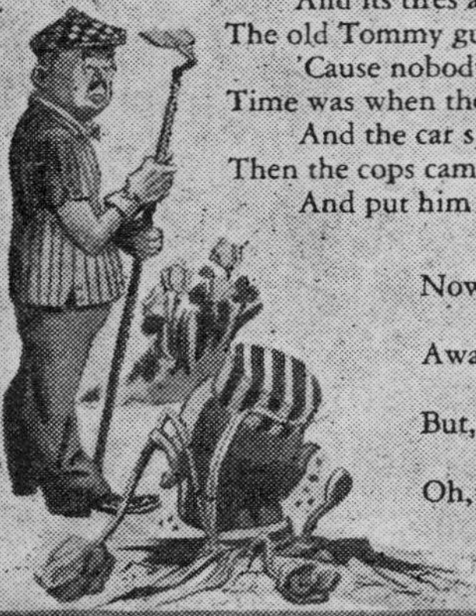

Now the gun and the car in silence stand,
Each one in the same old place,
Awaiting the touch of his grubby hand,
And the snarl on his ugly face.
But, alas, no more are his footsteps heard
In this outside world of strife.
Oh, what has become of Killer Boy Furd
Since they put him away for life?

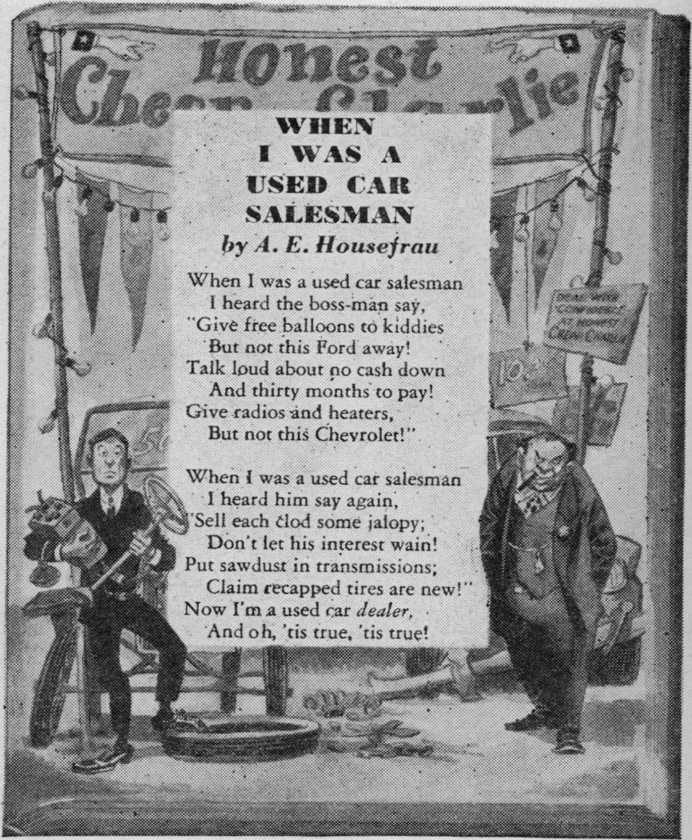
Honest

# WHEN I WAS A USED CAR SALESMAN

*by A. E. Housefrau*

When I was a used car salesman
I heard the boss-man say,
"Give free balloons to kiddies
But not this Ford away!
Talk loud about no cash down
And thirty months to pay!
Give radios and heaters,
But not this Chevrolet!"

When I was a used car salesman
I heard him say again,
"Sell each clod some jalopy;
Don't let his interest wain!
Put sawdust in transmissions;
Claim recapped tires are new!"
Now I'm a used car *dealer,*
And oh, 'tis true, 'tis true!

END

LADIES OF DISTINCTION DEPT.

Several months ago, the powers that be in Advertising decided to permit the use of women in whiskey ads. Of course, things will probably go slow in this new and touchy area. At first, women will only be used as props,

# WOMEN

# IN

PICTURE BELOW SHOWS HOW WOMEN

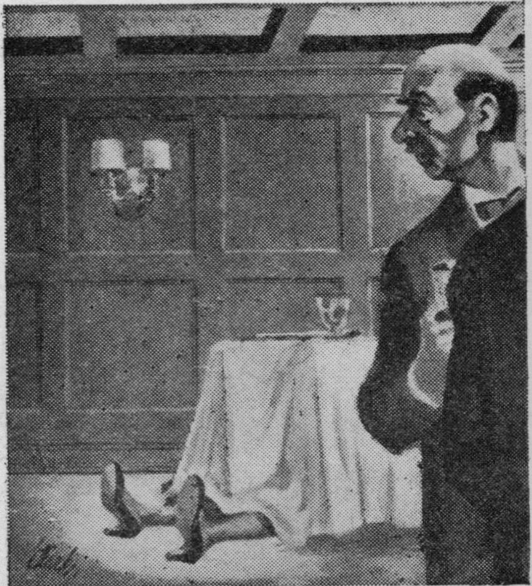

ON THE FOLLOWING PAGES, MAY APPEAR IN THE NEAR

standing around looking pretty. But as time goes on, and people get used to the idea, the fair sex will be shown taking a nip or two. Here, then, is MAD's idea of what the future holds, as Madison Avenue introduces . . .

# WHISKEY ADS

**ARE SUBTLY BEING INTRODUCED INTO WHISKEY ADS**

**MAD PRESENTS A DISPLAY OF HOW WHISKEY ADS FUTURE. MAINLY, MAD PRESENTS THEM SIDEWAYS LIKE THIS . . .**

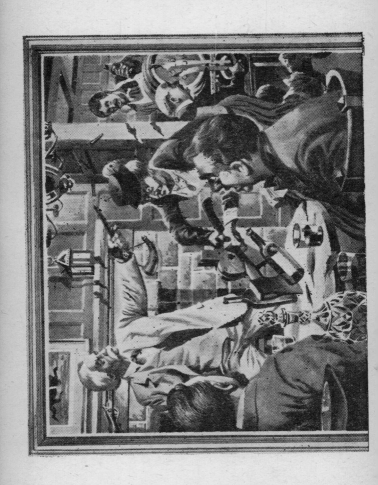

## Carrie Nation starts her Bar-Wrecking Crusade

Wit flashed when Mark Twain spoke and his favorite Kentucky bourbon, Old Crow, flowed during the convivial evenings at his favorite tavern. Except for the time that famed Prohibitionist started hacking up the place. Then, he wasn't very witty. In fact, he was downright abusive!

Taste the Greatness of

## OLD CROW

America's Preferred Bourbon

Yes, in the past, a few women like Carrie Nation disapproved of Old Crow. But today, more and more women are singing its praise. Of course, they may still hack up the place, but only because they get loaded on this famous Kentucky bourbon.

*"The Greatest Name in Bourbon"*

141

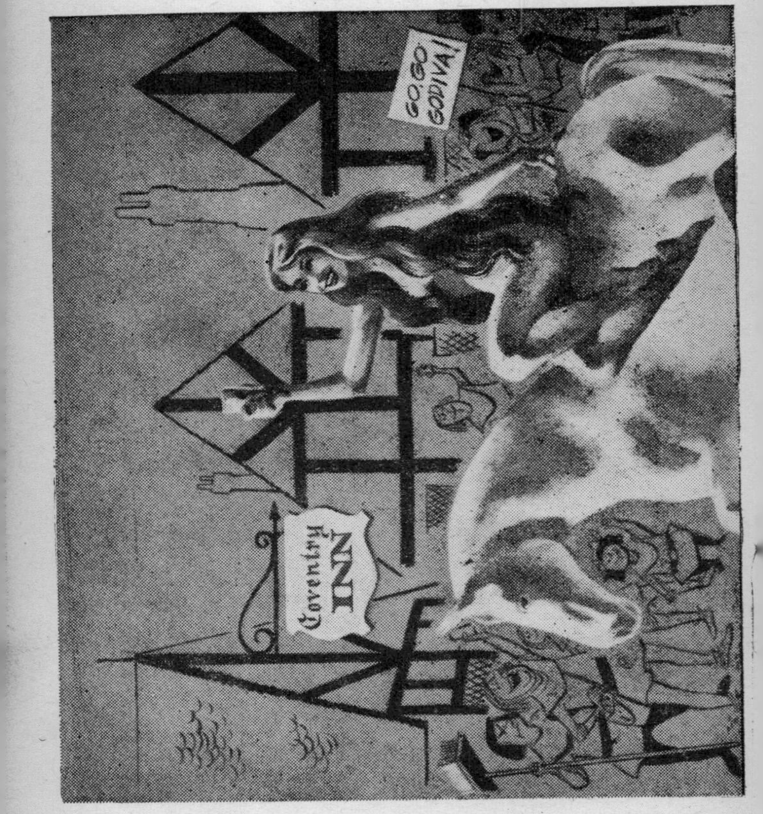
GO GO GODIVA!
Coventry INN

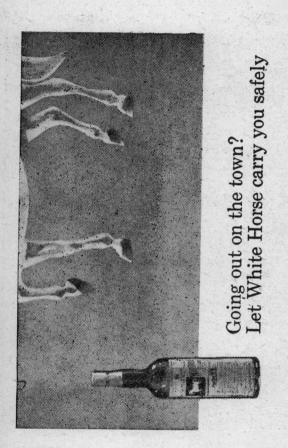

Going out on the town?
Let White Horse carry you safely

Another adventure in one of the 87 lands where Canadian Club is "Busting Up The House"

**WHISPERING CAMPAIGN** is begun about newly-arrived tea-drinkers.

**WORD SPREADS** about new folks concerning their addiction to tea.

TEETOTALING NEW NEIGHBOR menaces status quo of girl friends of Canadian Club, who gather to decide what to do about her.

TORCHLIGHT PARADE runs dope-fiend family quickly out of town.

*The Whiskey of Adventurous Lushes*

# BACKYARD BACKSTABBING

### HOW THE GIRLS GOT RID OF STICK-IN-THE-MUD NEW ARRIVALS

"We certainly took care of those kill-joys!" writes a girl friend of Canadian Club in an illegible scrawl. Yes, there are girl friends of Canadian Club just like there are boy friends of Canadian Club! These are folks who travel the world over, searching for adventure. And it isn't long before they find themselves doing adventurous things like riding wild boars bareback, or fighting rhinoceroses with ping-pong paddles. They do this, not because they are brave, but because they get so tanked up with Canadian Club, they don't even realize what they are doing! So why wait? Become a friend of

*Canadian Club*

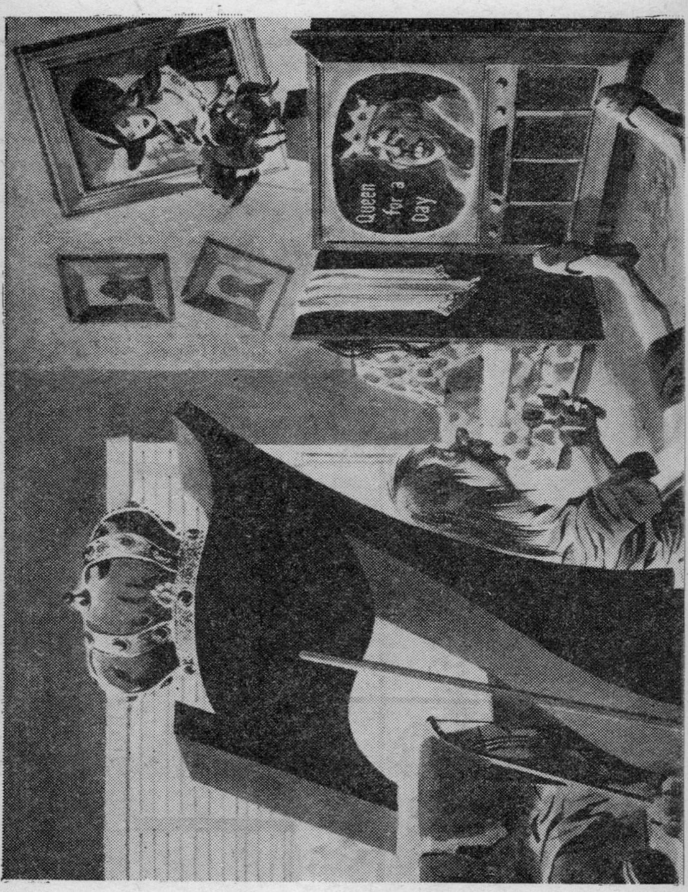
Queen for a day

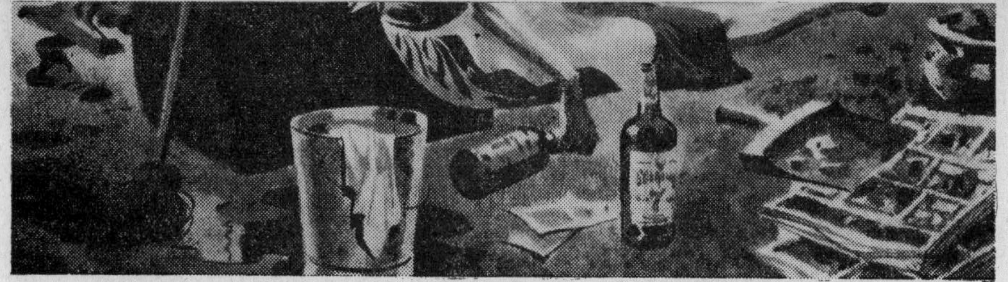

# LEISURE TIME U.S.A.

## WITH Seagram's 7 Crown

Leisure time for husbands starts at 7 in the evening, when he gets home from the office and grabs himself a couple of quick belts. Wives, however, have a decided advantage. They can start their leisure time at 7 in the morning, just as soon as the bum leaves for work.

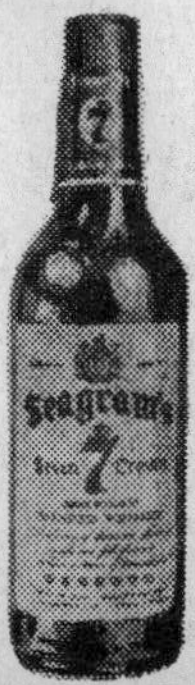
Seagram's
7

# EVENTUALLY, EVEN THE NAMES OF THE WHISKEYS WILL BE CHANGED

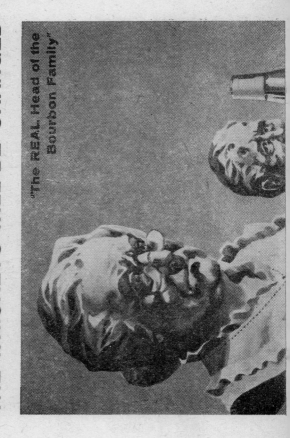

"The REAL Head of the Bourbon Family"

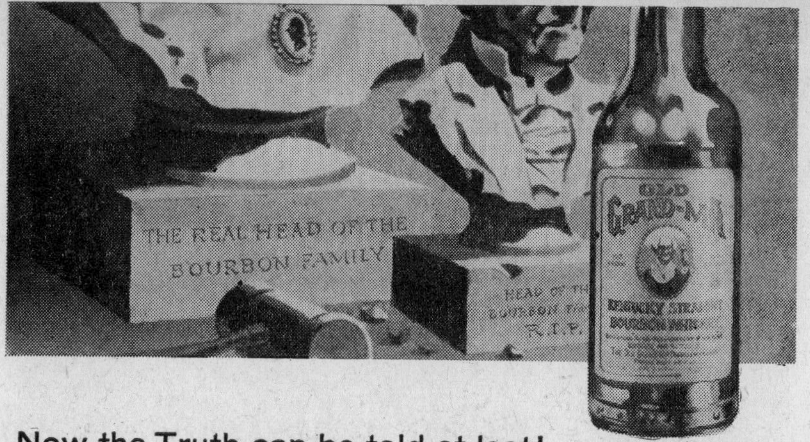
THE REAL HEAD OF THE
BOURBON FAMILY
R.I.P.
OLD
GRAND-MA
KENTUCKY STRAIGHT
BOURBON WHISKEY

## Now the Truth can be told at last!

It's about time that those namby-pamby Madison Avenue Martini-Sippers got around to letting us women take our rightful place in these whiskey ads. For years, *this* old fraud has been passing himself off as the big wheel in Kentucky bourbon. Well, I'm mighty glad to set the record straight. I hope that, now, other patriotic gals will step forward and show who the *real guzzlers in the family are!*

# OLD GRAND MA

# AND THE NEXT LOGICAL STEP...
# CHILDREN IN WHISKEY ADS

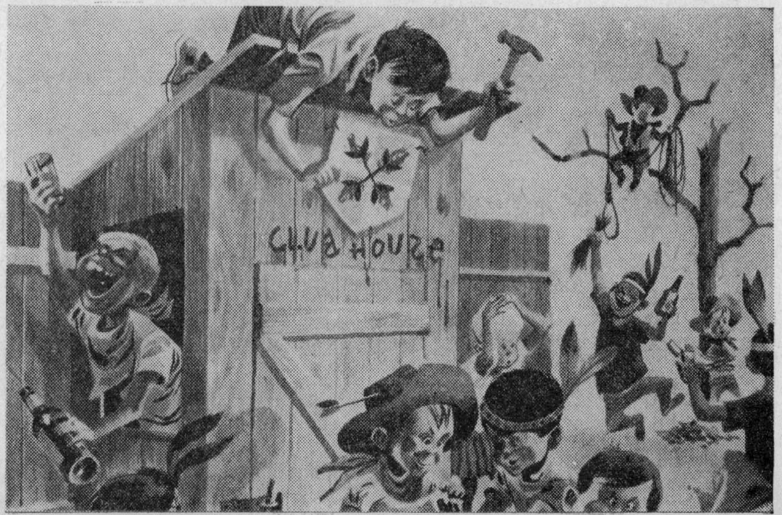
CLUB HOUSE

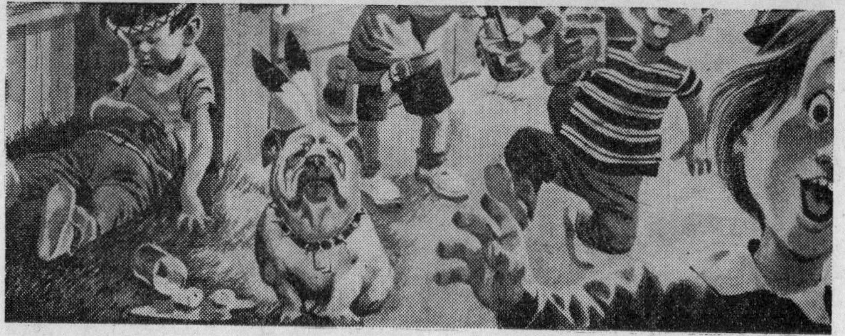

## THE JR. FOUR ROSES SOCIETY holds its first meeting

*(The Sly Little Nippers!)*

These kids really had themselves a ball after one of them got hold of his old man's bottle of booze. Namely, Four Roses—the whiskey that inspired a game of *Cowboys 'n Indians* like it never was played before. After that came a game of *Blind Man's Buff* where everybody was "it" because everybody was "blind". And as a topper, they tried *Pin-The-Tail-On-The-Pink-Elephant*. Get your kids to form a Junior Four Roses Society. It keeps them off the streets and out of trouble.

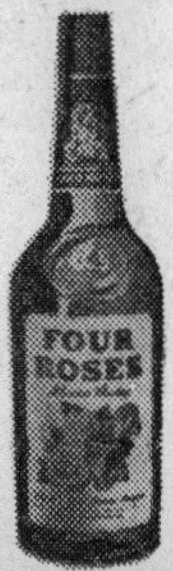
FOUR
ROSES

**FOUR ROSES** *The Full-Quart Whiskey for Half-Pint Alcoholics*

END

# IN SURGERY

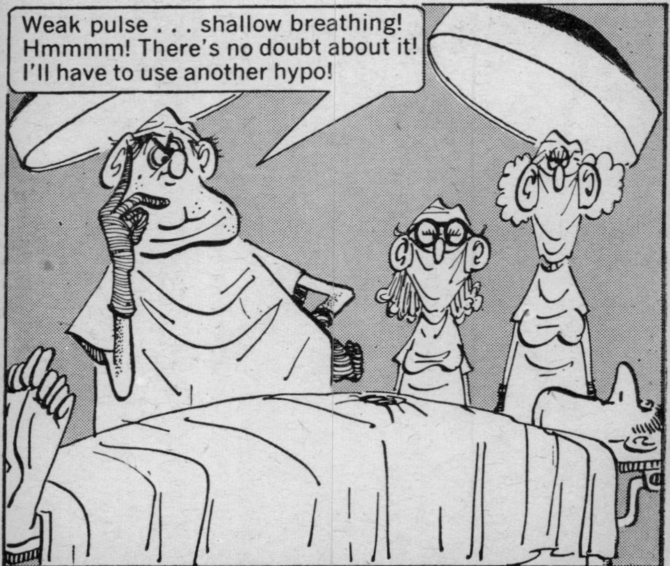
Weak pulse . . . shallow breathing!
Hmmmm! There's no doubt about it!
I'll have to use another hypo!

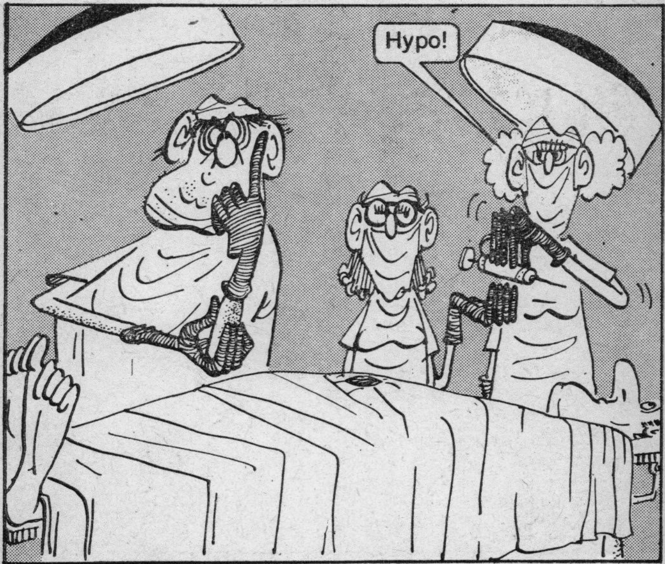
Hypo!

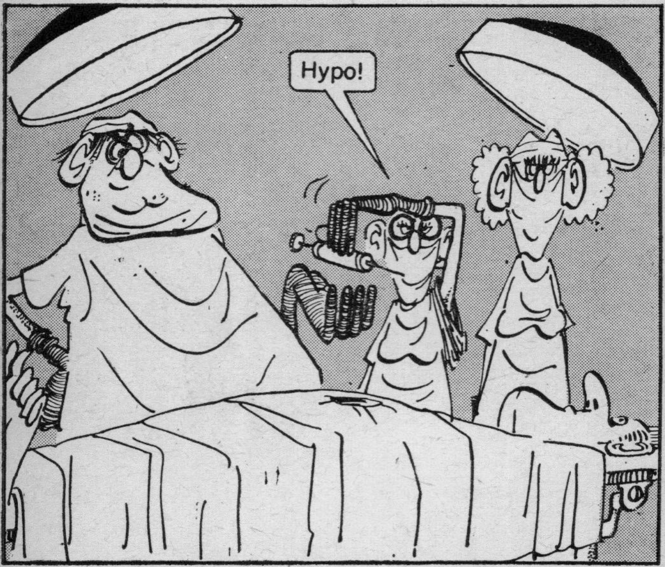
Hypo!

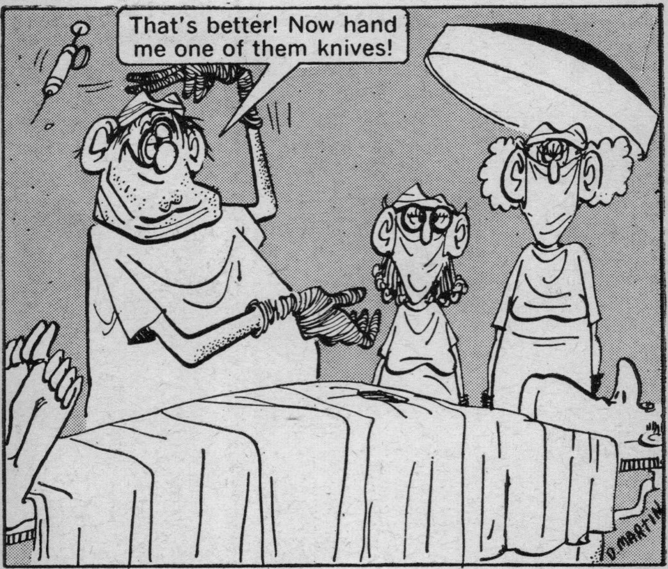
That's better! Now hand me one of them knives!
D. MARTIN

**END**

## POMP-ADORE DEPT.

We've got a confession to make! Confession being: MAD is not the funniest magazine on the newsstands today! There are magazines that are much funnier! Mainly, those serious magazines for "Teenagers"! You'll see what we mean if you study this typical example called . . .

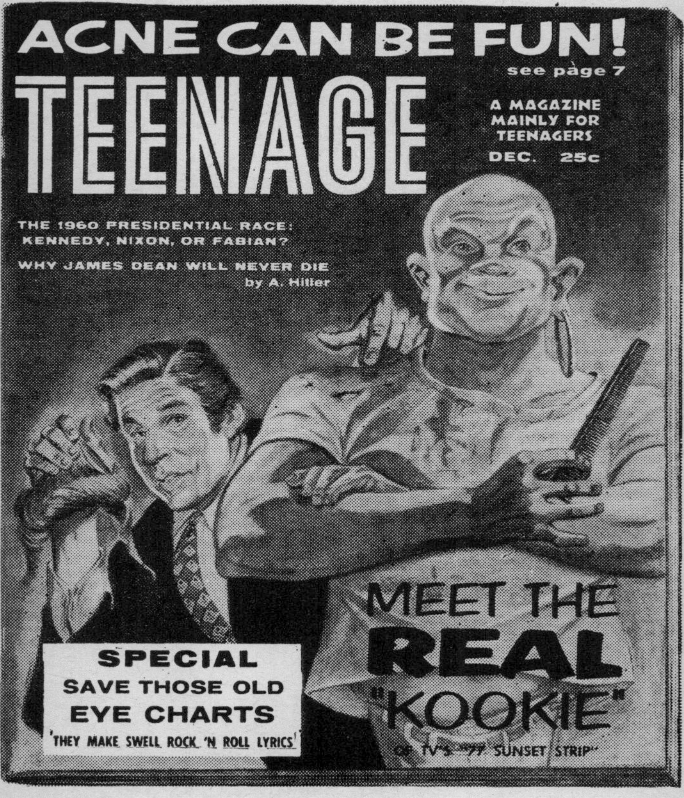

ACNE CAN BE FUN!
see page 7
TEENAGE
A MAGAZINE MAINLY FOR TEENAGERS
DEC. 25c
THE 1960 PRESIDENTIAL RACE: KENNEDY, NIXON, OR FABIAN?
WHY JAMES DEAN WILL NEVER DIE by A. Hitler
SPECIAL
SAVE THOSE OLD EYE CHARTS
'THEY MAKE SWELL ROCK 'N ROLL LYRICS'
MEET THE REAL "KOOKIE"
TV'S "77 SUNSET STRIP"

TEENAGE MAGAZINE PRESENTS:

# Teenager of the Month

## 15-YEAR-OLD MURRAY BLECH

*Once again, TEENAGE Magazine's Ace Photographer, Ninny Sklar, takes you on a pictorial journey through a typical day in the life of a typical teenager. Our typical teenager this month is fifteen-year-old Murray Blech . . .*

**UP AT 7:00 A.M.,** Murray combs his hair until 9:15. Then he combs his sideburns until 11:00. At 11:01, he'll sit down with his guitar and compose his daily Rock 'n Roll song. At 11:08, Murray will record the song on his home recorder. At 11:14, his own record company, *Compost Discs,* will press it, and release it. By noon, it will sell a million copies . . .

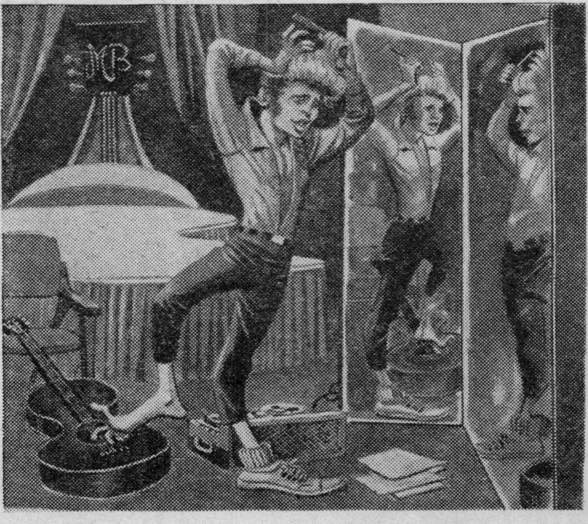

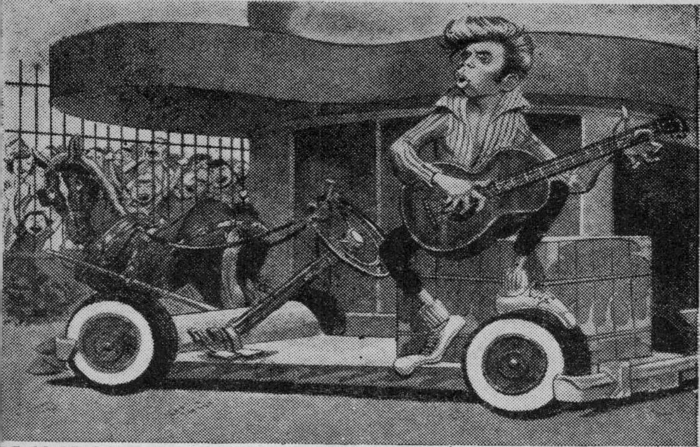

**AT 12:15,** Murray is out in the backyard, puttering around his real gone custom car until 3:30. You'd never believe it, but that car Murray is standing next to was once a 1960 Cadillac. All the ingenious Murray did was nose it, deck it, lower it 12 inches, and throw away the engine, the brakes, the transmission and the chassis. Then he hitched a pony on the front to pull it. You'd never believe it, but that pony was once a horse. All the ingenious Murray did was nose him, deck him, lower him 12 inches, and throw away some skin, bones and hair. Any of you guys and gals can do the same thing!

**AT 4:00 O'CLOCK** Murray is at the Bandstand Show (natch), dancing with a real cool chick. He loves the other kids at the show because they're loads of fun, and not the least bit self-conscious about being on TV. Murray hasn't missed one afternoon dancing on The Bandstand Show in two-and-a-half years... an amazing record, considering the Show is in Philadelphia . . . and Murray lives out in Oregon.

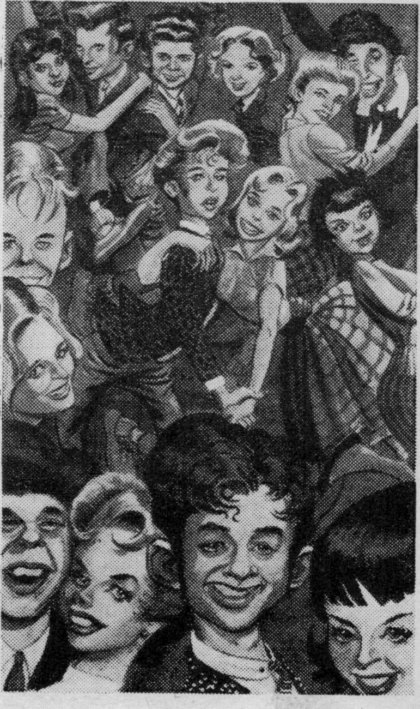

**AT 8:00 P.M.** Murray and his chick (his steady, natch)
attend a triple horror show at the Drive-In. They aren't
horrified at any of the feature films. They're horrified
at the musical short, in which a Rock 'n Roll singer has
accidentally hit a clinker . . . and pronounced a real un-
derstandable English word! After taking his chick home,
Murray will return to his own house at 2:00 AM! He will
comb his hair and sideburns until 4:00 AM and then retire.

*And so ends a busy day in the life of*

*TEENAGE Magazine's "Teenager of the Month,"*

*Murray Blech. Of course, tomorrow being Saturday,*

*and no school, he'll be able to relax . . .*

# PENMATES

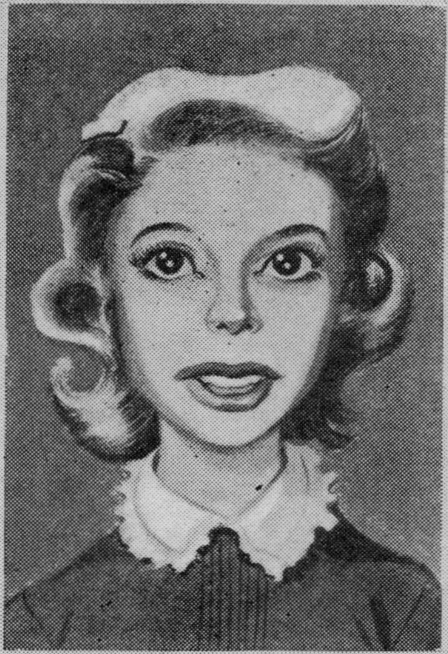

*I'd love to hear from boys 16-19. I'm 15, and have brown hair and blue eyes. I love dancing, Elvis, Ricky, Dick, Sal, Pat, Tommy, Fabian, James Dean, hot rods, short shorts, pop records, stock cars and my mother, in that order.

Phoebe Newt
142 S. Green
Stronghead, Montana

\*I'm a cool widow of 14. My late husband and I used to dance on the bandstand show. He was killed while we were fighting nine other couples for a good camera position. I'd sure like to meet another cute guy of 15. But not for another week. After all, how would it look?

Yetta Blintzner
185 Carter St.
Littleliver Pill, North Dakota

*Hi, everybody! I just arrived, and I'm lonesome! I'm 18. I love hot rods. My favorite relaxation is playing "chicken" at 110 MPH. Am anxious to hear from Jimmy Dean and the rest of the wild bunch who made it here before me.
     Monty Monroe
     Block 4, Row D.
     Forest Lawn Cemetery
     Los Angeles, California

*I'm 16, 5' 8", 162 lbs., and I have brown wavy hair, green eyes, a sparkling smile, dimples, broad shoulders, a slim waist, and well-muscled arms and legs. Actually, I don't want to meet anybody. I just love to describe myself!
  Myron Gorzz
  No address given

*Hi, there. I'd like to meet a nice, settled, serious-minded teen-age girl. I have a great sense of humor, and I'm loads of fun at large dinners and funerals.

        G. Jessel
        Hollywood, California

*I'm a lonely fellow who is quite short. Although I'm 17, I'm only 4' 3" tall. I'd like to meet a nice short chick. Or if not, maybe 53 other guys my height to help me set a new telephone booth-stuffing record.

Steve Vonce
88 Skincondition Street
Noxema, Vermont

# Dear Seymour

*If you have a question you'd like answered, address a letter to* Dear Seymour, c/o TEENAGE, Ira's Candy Store, Palo Alto, Calif. *All correspondence will be treated with utmost discretion, but we ask that you include your name and address, your phone number and your picture. All letters become the property of* TEENAGE. *All teenagers become the property of Seymour if he likes your looks.*

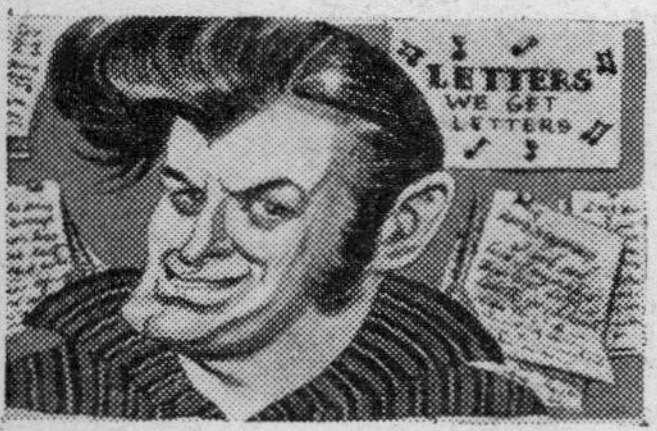
LETTERS
WE GET LETTERS

Dear Seymour:

I'm sick and tired of immature teenage boys. I'd like to go out with an older fellow. I was thinking of calling Carl Sandburg for a date next Saturday; and also asking him if he has a friend for my friend. What do you think?

Birdie,
Chicago, Ill.

**I think you're quite immature, and have a lot to learn about dating, and life in general! Your idea is childish and completely ridiculous! After all, why drag a friend along on a first date?*

Dear Seymour:

I am 13 years old, and have only recently learned about kissing. I must admit that I am a bit confused. For example, is kissing my mother "different" from kissing a date?

Irving
Brooklyn, N. Y.

**I'm afraid I can't answer that for you, Irving. I've never kissed your mother!*

Dear Seymour:

I am 17, very pretty, and come from a good family. Recently I met a fellow who is 19, very handsome, has a car, a good job, and also comes from a good family. We are engaged to be married, and are very happy. What I'd like to know is: how can I have problems like other teenagers?

Muriel
Montclair, N. J.

**Join clubs, develop new interests, meet new people, and above all . . . be yourself!*

Dear Seymour:

Do you think it's all right for a 15-year old teenage girl to go away for a month with a married man to a cabin in Maine, and go out with him to bars every night?

Goldie
St. Louis, Mo.

**Yes, providing you're back in the cabin no later than 10:00 P.M. on school nights.*

Dear Seymour:

I have a terrible teenage problem, and if someone doesn't solve it for me, I'll go out of my mind. Here I am, going on 14, and I still haven't written or recorded a single Rock 'n Roll hit song. Is there something terribly wrong with me?

Marvin
Sarasota, Fla.

**Yes!*

Dear Seymour:

My wife is a nice average teen-age girl, and we have two average teenage children, the older of which is jealous of the younger. Anyway, last month my car was stolen, and ever since it happened, my wife has refused to date me. She insists that no average teenage girl dates a fellow without a car. This is maddening. Please advise.

Bernie
Absalom, N. C.

*Stop worrying. Show your older child as much love as you show your younger, and he won't be jealous anymore!*

Dear Seymour:

How come you never answer questions with funny jokes, like "Abby" and "Ann" do?

Klaus,
White Sands, N. M.

*How's this? The best way to drive a baby buggy is tickle his feet!*

Dear Seymour:

You call that a funny joke?

Klaus,
White Sands, N. M.

*Why don't you ask funny questions like "Abby" and "Ann's" readers do?*

# DISKVILLE
## LATEST RECORD NEWS
### by
### Sheldon "Groovy" Abisch

♭ ♭ *There's no short cut to fame in pop music!* Take that exciting new vocal group, **THE BARNYARDERS.** These four swinging young plumbers' apprentices from Decatur, Illinois, were singing together for nearly two and a half weeks before they made it!

♮ ♮ *Have you dug the sensaysh new platter,* "The Belly-Roll Rock-a-Billy Boogie Cha Cha Boogie Billy-a-Rock Roll Belly"? Lyrics for this great new tune, in case you don't know, were written by **BING CROSBY'S** new teenage son, **HARRY!** He's 15! Months, that is . . . and a real comer!

♭ ♭ It looks like that great Rock 'n Roll Singer, **FABIAN**, will join **KING ELVIS, PAT, RICKY**, and **SAL** as a movie star. A talent scout from **20th**, heard **FABE'S** new smasheroo waxing of "Rockin' at the Taj Mahal", and signed him immediately for a juicy role in the new flick based on the life of **DR. JONAS SALK.** Handsome **FABE** will play a swinging teenage heart specialist. Good luck, **FABE!**

♮ ♮ *Betcha can't guess what R 'n R great* **FRANKIE AVALON** is planning to do with the royalties from his fabulous new disc, "My Teenage Lips Are Chapped From Kissing an Ice Cold Chick"! **FRANKIE's** going to buy the British Isles. Smart move, **FRANKIE!**

♭ ♭ There's no stopping **RICKY NELSON** these days. The Dee Jays tell me he now has 43 platters in "The Top Ten"! Good work, **RICKI**

♮ ♮ **RUMORSVILLE:** No matter what you may hear, there is *no truth* to the rumor that **FABIAN** and **LEONARD BERNSTEIN** are feuding! We've also checked the rumor that **THE FLEETWOODS, THE BONNEVILLES, THE IMPALAS, THE CADILLACS, THE CORVETTES**, and **THE ELDORADOS** Vocal Groups are backed by General Motors, and it's *definitely not true!* They're backed by Chrysler!

♭ ♭ **PLATTERS TO WATCH** (but not to listen to): "Tired Teenage Feet in Dirty Teenage Sneakers" by **THE SNORERS** on the Swill Label; "The Edward G. Robinson Rock" by **JACK LARUE** on the Flybynight Label; "That Teenage Grandma of Mine" by **NICKY KHRUSHCHEV** on the Red Label; The "Gazzadzt Gdflg Ooh-Ah Mnf Cha Cha Cha" by **THE SPEECH MAJORS** on the Iodinebottle Label.

♮ ♮ **NEWCOMERS:** Watch for an exciting new song writer named Cole Porter! One of his tunes made the Number 98 spot all over the country this week, despite the fact that it is not R 'n R. And they tell me Cole isn't even a teenager! Which proves that there's truly opportunity for all here in the good ol' rockin' U.S.A.!

# How Much Do You Know About KISSING?

### by Sonia Schlepp
### TEENAGE Magazine's Kissing Editor

*How much do you teenage teenagers know about kissing? Sonia Schlepp, our Kissing Editor, has devised this special quiz so you can find out. Simply answer the following statements True or False. The correct answer with an explanation follows each statement.*

**(1) IT IS BEST TO KISS A GIRL WITH YOUR EYES CLOSED.**

False. It is best to kiss a girl with your lips!

**(2) YOU CAN LEARN A LOT ABOUT KISSING FROM A GOOD HYGIENE BOOK.**

True. But it's not much fun kissing a Hygiene book!

**(3) KISSING IN A PARKED CAR CAN GIVE A GIRL A BAD REPUTATION.**

True. Unless she's with a boy!

**(4) IF YOU TRY TO KISS A GIRL THE FIRST TIME YOU GO OUT WITH HER, SHE WILL LOSE RESPECT FOR YOU, AND SHE WON'T GO OUT WITH YOU AGAIN.**

True. Perhaps the following example will illustrate. Several months ago there was a fire in my house. As I dashed into the hall, a fireman appeared, picked me up, and said, "C'mon, Miss, I'll take you out!" We dashed out into the street seconds before the building collapsed. He was so happy we were safe, he tried to kiss me. Since it was the first time he'd taken me out, I naturally turned him down. What's more, I lost respect for him. And he later regretted his action, too. Because every fire after that, I went out with another fireman!

**(5) A KISS ON THE HAND MAY BE QUITE CONTINENTAL.**

True. But diamonds are a girl's best friend!

**(6) THINKING ABOUT KISSING TOO MUCH CAN BE HARMFUL.**

True. Let me cite the case of a teen-ager who spent a whole day thinking about kissing. The same evening, he died as a result of severe electrical damage to his brain. He would not have died that evening if he had not thought about kissing all day, and if the Governor's reprieve had arrived at the Death House in time!

**(7) TOO MUCH THINKING ABOUT HUGGING CAN BE HARMFUL.**

I haven't the slightest idea! I'm TEENAGE Magazine's Kissing Editor!

## NEW

# TEENAGE MAGAZINE'S FREE ALL-IN-ONE FAN CLUB

Hey, guys and gals! Tired of joining a hundred different clumsy and involved FAN CLUBS? How about joining **one** single different clumsy and involved FAN CLUB? We're talking about TEENAGE Magazine's NEW **FREE** ALL-IN-ONE FAN CLUB! It's absolutely **FREE,** and it's one of the few really legitimate fan club organizations not run by a fly-by-night company. All you have to do to join is send your name and address to: TEENAGE Magazine's New **FREE** All-In-One Fan Club, c/o Ira's Candy Store, Palo Alto. Calif. Remember, this ALL-IN-ONE FAN CLUB is absolutely **FREE!**

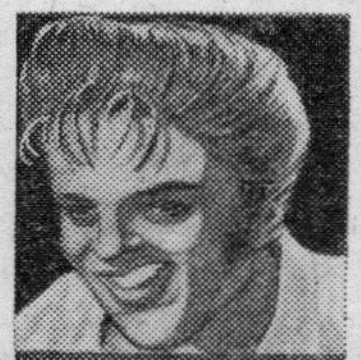

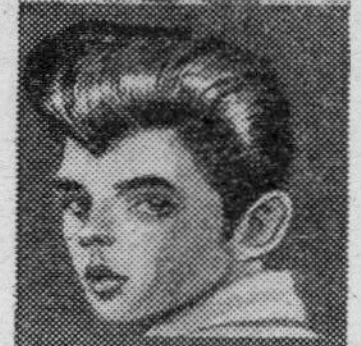

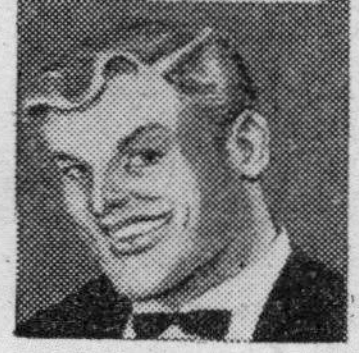

**UPON JOINING EVERY MEMBER RECEIVES ABSOLUTELY FREE:**

1. A beautiful All-In-One Fan Club Membership Card.
2. 8 Beautiful full-size photos of Elvis, Ricky, Sal, Tab, Fabian, etc.
3. 8 wallet-size photos of Elvis, Ricky, Sal, Tab, Fabian, etc.
4. 8 photo-size shots of the wallets of Elvis, Ricky, Sal, Tab, Fabian, etc.
5. A beautiful candid photo of Elvis, Ricky, Sal, Tab, Fabian, and all the other R 'n R stars in a scene from their new all-in-one movie, "A Hundred Men in Search of a Voice."
6. A gorgeous composite wallet-size blow-up photo of all the members of the families of Elvis, Ricky, Sal, Tab, Fabian, etc., as children

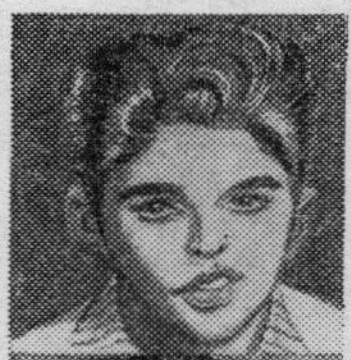

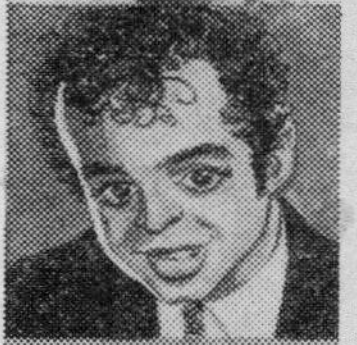

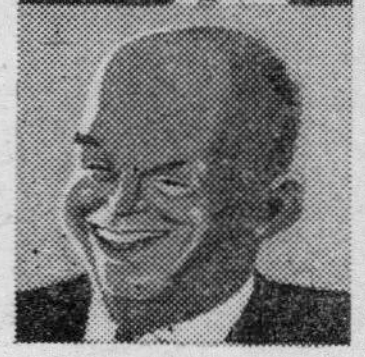

**REGISTRATION FEE** (during a solar eclipse, if it should occur on Leap Year Day, and Grand Central Station is empty between the hours of 7:00 AM and Noon)....25¢
**ALL OTHER TIMES** ....................................................$175

**BONUS:** A Beautiful 8 x 10 Glossy Photo of Secretary of Agriculture Ezra Taft Benson as a teenager!

**EXTRA BONUS:** A beautiful 8 x 10 Glossy Photograph of Bing Crosby's new son, Harry . . . as an adult!

**SENSATIONAL EXTRA BONUS:** Every reader who joins this fan club, and sends all the money required to: TEENAGE Magazine's New **FREE** All-In-One Fan Club, c/o Ira's Candy Store, Palo Alto, Calif., will receive a beautiful 8 x 10 Glossy Photo of Ira's Candy Store being blown up to make room for the new Freeway, and the editors of this magazine scurrying off to a Brazil-bound plane with sacks of money.



END

We understand there's a big commotion going on in England these days—which brings us to this article. (And we're not talking about the commotion going on in England over MAD. That's another article!) We're talking about the commotion over the way writers, and particularly American advertising agencies, are parodying and altering revered Gilbert and Sullivan operettas for personal profits. Well, we've got news for our British cousins. When American advertising agencies latch onto something, they never let go! As a matter of fact, things can only get worse. Especially when . . .

# MADISON AVENUE TURNS to HISTORY AND LITERATURE

Here's an ad based on the works of **William Shakespeare**

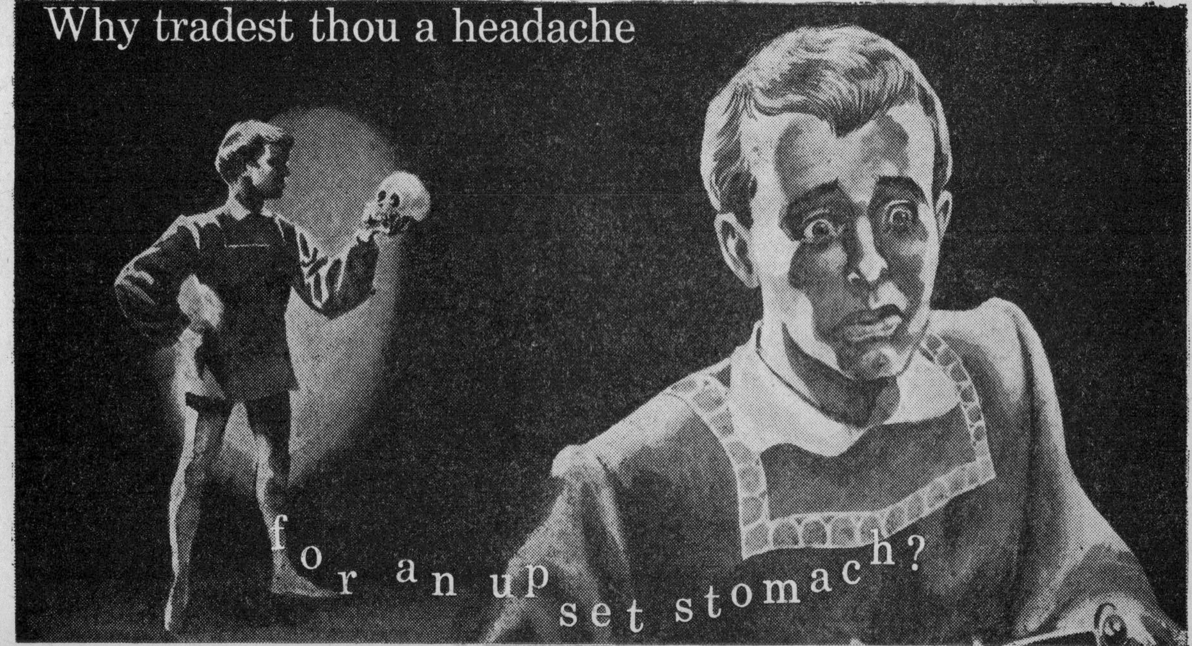
Why tradest thou a headache
for an upset stomach?

# When thou takest Bufferin, pain exeunts at-the-nonce

"When empty, this bottle may be filled with poison for application to kings' ears."

To take **B**, or not to take **B**,
That is the question.
Whether 'tis nobler in the mind to suffer
The stings and sorrows of outrageous cold misery,
And then, like a fool, to take aspirin against a sea of neuralgia,
And by opposing, not end it, but perhaps thyself.
To die, to sleep no more from aspirin's *acetylsalicylic acid*,
Or if thou art fortunate, at the very best to feel queasy and sick,
And with this aspirin, accelerate the muscular aches,
The nerve-jangling, and the thousand natural shocks
That flesh is heir to.
Or to take Bufferin.
'Tis a consummation devoutly to be wished.
For with its anti-acid Di-Alminate*
(*Bristol-Myers' brand of aluminum glycinate and magnesium carbonate)
Not to die—but to sleep.
To sleep blissfully—perchance to dream.—
And not have to trade in thy headache for an upset stomach,
And therefore not have to undergo unnecessary abdominal massage,
Aye, with Bufferin, there's no rub!

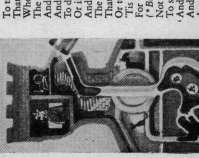

173

This ad copy makes use of a poem by **Edgar Allan Poe**

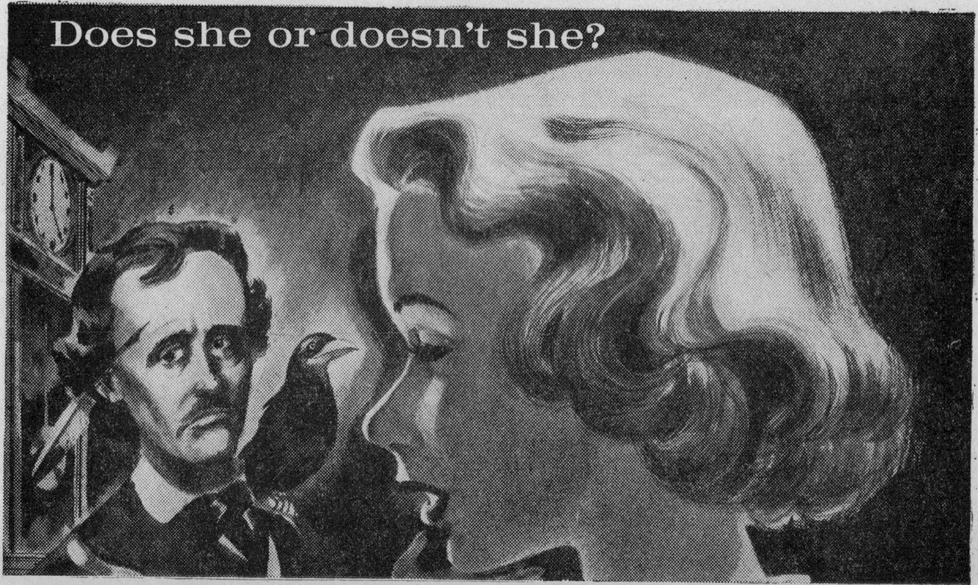
Does she or doesn't she?

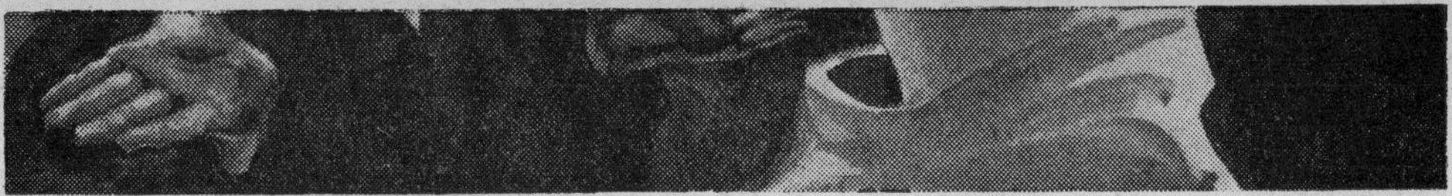

## Hair Color so natural only her hairdresser knows for sure!

It was many and many a year ago,
In a kingdom by the sea
That a maiden with hair color natural lived
By the name of MISS CLAIROL LEE;
And I lived in those days with no other thought
Than: Does she or doesn't she?

I was a child and she was a child,
In this kingdom by the sea,
And all of the children were dyeing their hair—
But what of MISS CLAIROL LEE?
And I wondered as she stroked my purple-green locks:
Does she or doesn't she?

But then one day a hairdresser came
To our kingdom by the sea;
And he marveled at the beautiful silky strands
Of my own, my MISS CLAIROL LEE.
And I said to him, "Please, Mr. Hairdresser, Sir—
Does she or doesn't she?"

Then he was gone and she was gone
From our kingdom by the sea.
And one day I heard that the angels above
Had taken my MISS CLAIROL LEE.
And now, only God and that hairdresser knows—
Did she or didn't she?

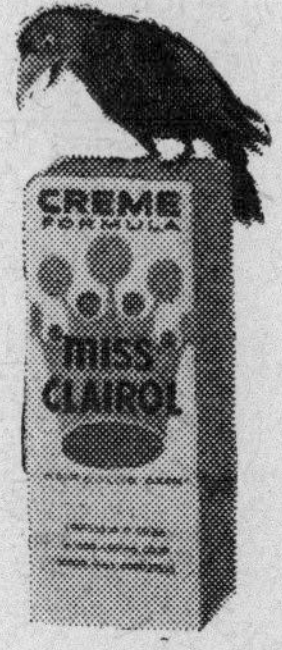
CREME
FORMULA
MISS CLAIROL

Here's an advertisement which parodies **Carl Sandburg**

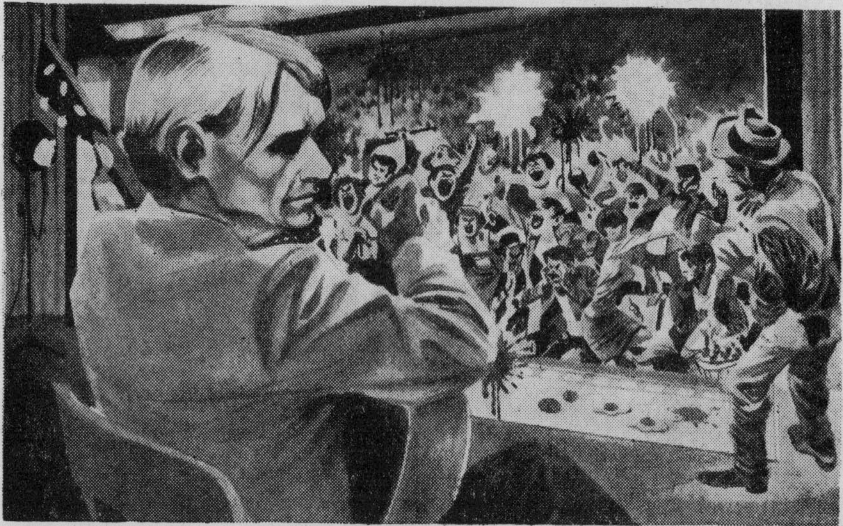

# TOOTHPASTE MAKER FOR THE WORLD

## DECAY FIGHTER, CREATOR OF THE INVISIBLE PROTECTIVE SHIELD

**Brushing...Cleaning...Sweetening...**

# I AM COLGATE

## CONQUEROR OF THE NATION'S BAD BREATH!

They tell me you have mouth odor and I believe them; for I have seen your painted women laugh at you through their gas masks.
They tell me you have tooth decay, and I answer: "Yes, I have seen you visit your dentist 244 times a year."
And having answered, I say: "Lift up your head to the sun and flourish the blackness of your dentures, and accept my
Strength,
Vigor,
Stamina,
GARDOL."
Rub, scrub, scour, scrape.
Abrade, massage, rasp, draw blood.
Through the haze, under the smoke, amid the blackness, a Gardol protective shield building.
To protect you from bad breath? Perhaps! And tooth decay? I think so!
But more important, to protect you from baseballs, and golfballs, and footballs, and horseshoes, and other TV accouterments.
I AM COLGATE.
Proud to be Toothpaste Maker for the World, Decay Fighter, Creator of the Invisible Protective Shield, Conqueror of the Nation's Bad Breath, Toothpaste of the Big Stock Dividend.

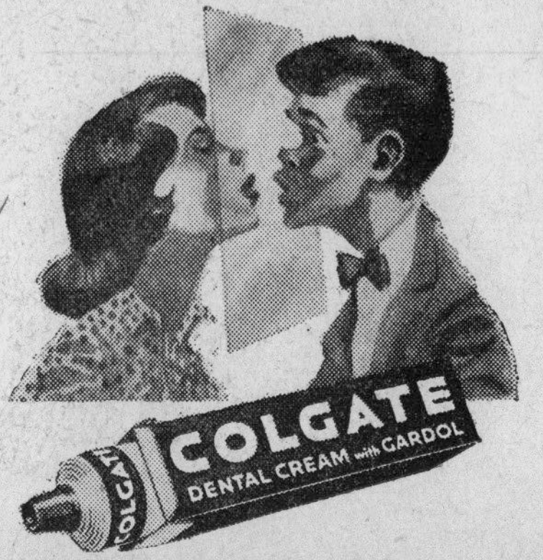
COLGATE
DENTAL CREAM with GARDOL
COLGATE

This advertisement slightly alters Abraham Lincoln

# With malice toward none
# With Filter-Blend for all

Four score and seven years ago, our company brought forth on this continent a new cigarette, conceived in choice tobaccos, and dedicated to the proposition that not all brands are created equal. Now we we are engaged in a great advertising war, testing whether our wishy-washy competitors with "Thinking Man's Filters" and "Live Modern Flavor" can long endure. We are met on a great battlefield of that war, this advertising space having cost us $45,000. We have come to dedicate a portion of our cigarette, that part which lies before our pure white filter, as a final proof that *it's what's up front that counts*. It is altogether fitting and proper that we should do this, for we are getting paid good money. But in a larger sense, we must now dedicate, we must now consecrate, we must now extol this cigarette more forcefully than ever. Our brave competitors, living and dead, have been feeding you a pack of lies. The world will little note, nor long remember what they've been saying, for they have lousy advertising agencies. But, we here highly resolve that this nation, under Winston, shall have a new birth of smokers, and that FILTER-BLEND of the cigarette, by the cigarette, and for the cigarette, shall not perish from our taste . . . *like a cigarette shouldn't!*

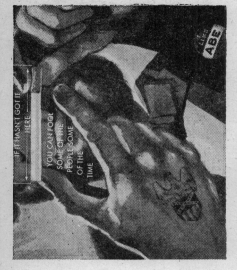

IF IT HASN'T GOT IT
HERE
YOU CAN FOOL SOME OF THE PEOPLE SOME OF THE TIME
ABE

KING SIZE
Winston
FILTER CIGARETTES
FINER FILTER FOR FINER FLAVOR

# Winston tastes good

***like you can't fool all of the people all of the time!***

END

## INSIDE PITCH DEPT.

*It seems as though the grey flannel set is getting desperate these days. Lately, everywhere you look—be it sides of busses, backs of menus, fronts of matchbooks, inside ball parks, outside ball parks, trash receptacles, beer coasters or roller coasters—you see an advertisement. Today, the ad men are searching frantically for any usable space which might be utilized for commercial pitches. We hear that even hotel room walls are being considered as spots where ads could be placed for greater impact. MAD foresees where it could all end if advertising men go for broke to get their message across in . . .*

# NEW
# AD

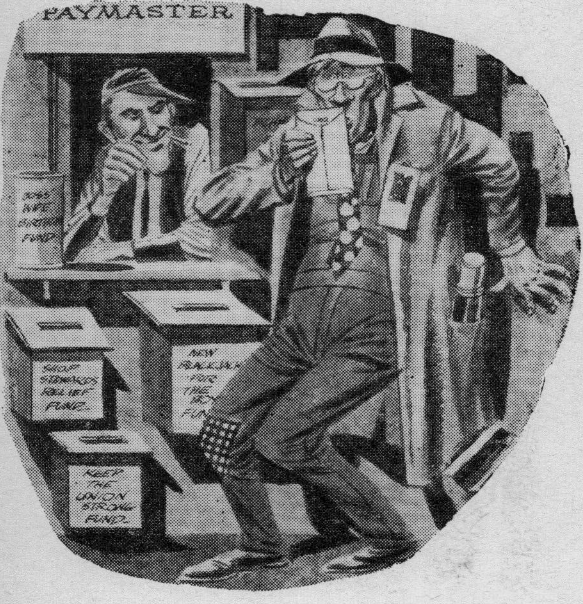
PAYMASTER
SHOP STEWARDS RELIEF FUND
KEEP THE UNION STRONG FUND

# SPACES

# IN BARROOMS

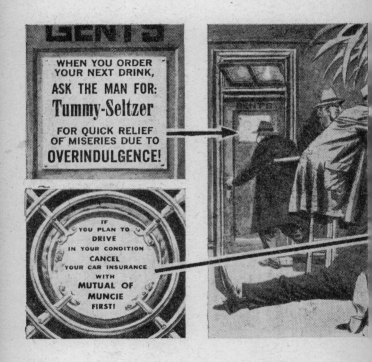

WHEN YOU ORDER YOUR NEXT DRINK, ASK THE MAN FOR: Tummy-Seltzer FOR QUICK RELIEF OF MISERIES DUE TO OVERINDULGENCE!

IF YOU PLAN TO DRIVE IN YOUR CONDITION CANCEL YOUR CAR INSURANCE WITH MUTUAL OF MUNCIE FIRST!

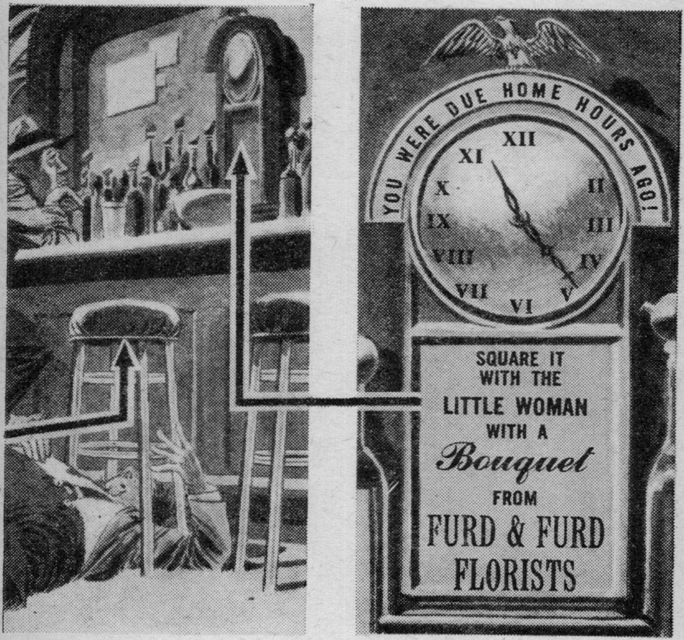
YOU WERE DUE HOME HOURS AGO!
XII
XI
X
II
IX
III
VIII
IV
VII
VI
V
SQUARE IT
WITH THE
LITTLE WOMAN
WITH A
Bouquet
FROM
FURD & FURD
FLORISTS

# IN PRISON CELLS

NEED TO REORGANIZE
YOUR OPERATION
FROM TOP TO BOTTOM
WHEN YOU'RE SPRUNG?

CALL

**APEX**

FOR

BONDED AND EXPERIENCED

- TORPEDOES
- GUN MOLLS
- STRONG ARM BOYS
- SAFE CRACKERS
- FINKS

**APEX**

EMPLOYMENT AGENCY

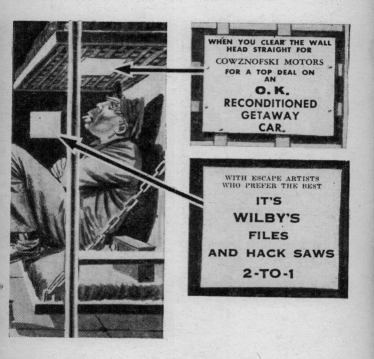

WHEN YOU CLEAR THE WALL
HEAD STRAIGHT FOR

COWZNOFSKI MOTORS

FOR A TOP DEAL ON
AN

O. K.
RECONDITIONED
GETAWAY
CAR.

WITH ESCAPE ARTISTS
WHO PREFER THE BEST

IT'S

WILBY'S

FILES

AND HACK SAWS

2-TO-1

# IN AIRLINERS

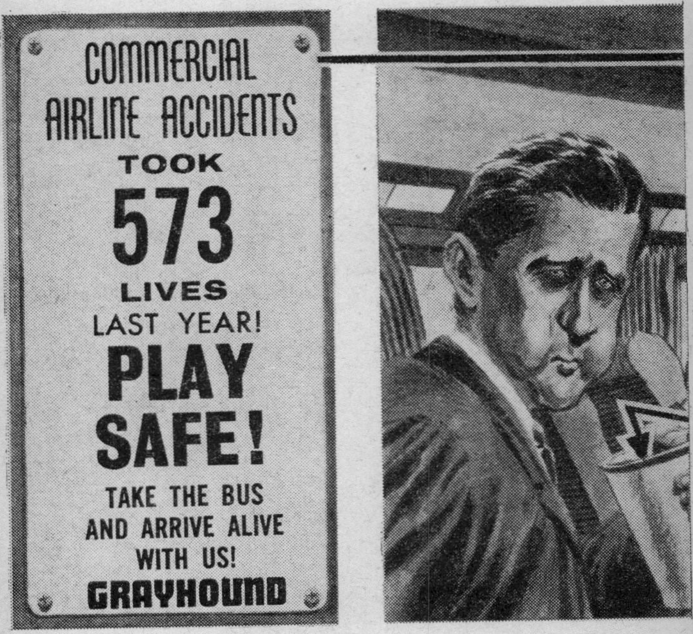

COMMERCIAL
AIRLINE ACCIDENTS
TOOK
**573**
LIVES
LAST YEAR!
# PLAY
# SAFE!
TAKE THE BUS
AND ARRIVE ALIVE
WITH US!
**GRAYHOUND**

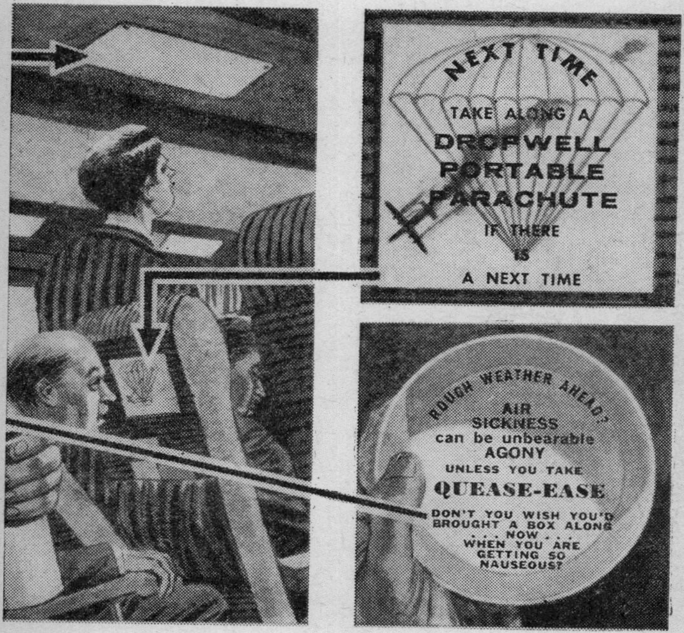
NEXT TIME
TAKE ALONG A
DROPWELL
PORTABLE
PARACHUTE
IF THERE
IS
A NEXT TIME
ROUGH WEATHER AHEAD?
AIR
SICKNESS
can be unbearable
AGONY
UNLESS YOU TAKE
QUEASE-EASE
DON'T YOU WISH YOU'D
BROUGHT A BOX ALONG
. . . NOW . . .
WHEN YOU ARE
GETTING SO
NAUSEOUS?

# ON PAY ENVELOPES

NORTH AMERICAN
VEEBLEFETZER CO.
PAY ENVELOPE

NAME: Ralph C. Wretched
SALARY: $90.00
DEDUCTIONS: $82.27
NET SALARY: $7.73

**SQUANDER IT ALL**
at
The Sitting Duck
**TAVERN**
Stop off on your way home, before the old crow gets her paws on it!

YOU CAN RUN THIS
**PITTANCE**
INTO A
**REAL BANKROLL**
AT
**DIRTY DAN'S**
FLOATING
CRAP GAME

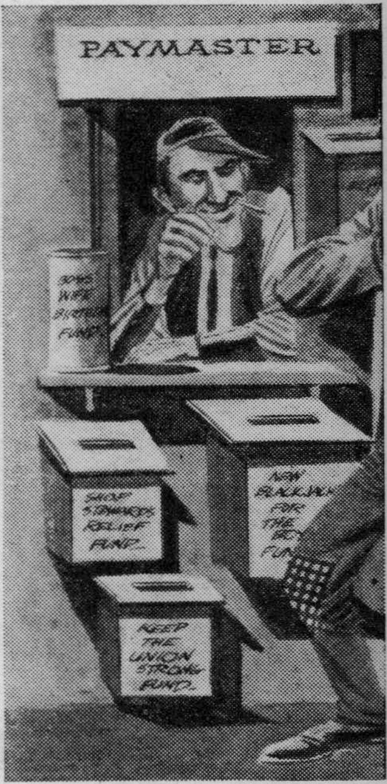
PAYMASTER
KEEP THE UNION STRONG FUND.

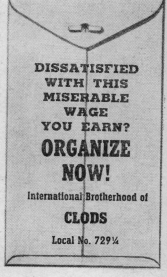

DISSATISFIED
WITH THIS
MISERABLE
WAGE
YOU EARN?

# ORGANIZE
# NOW!

International Brotherhood of

## CLODS

Local No. 729¼

# IN DRESSING ROOMS

Gain
Financial
Independence
BEFORE YOU'RE
TOO PUNCHY TO ENJOY IT!

**MAKE**
**BIG MONEY**

TAKING DIVES!
FOR DETAILS, CALL
LEW ESKIN'S
BOOKIE SYNDICATE
QU-3-3217
*(Ask for Big Lew)*

DON'T GO INTO THE RING
**DEFENSELESS!**
PACK EACH GLOVE WITH A
*Lucky Brand*
HORSESHOE
"Every One A Knockout!"
MADE OF FINEST TEMPERED
GERMAN STEEL

MAYBE YOU'D DO BETTER
IN THE
FLYWEIGHT CLASS!
**REDUCE**
THE MEDICALLY APPROVED WAY
at
VIC
LARDOFF'S

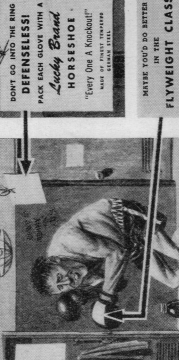

# IN HOSPITAL ROOMS

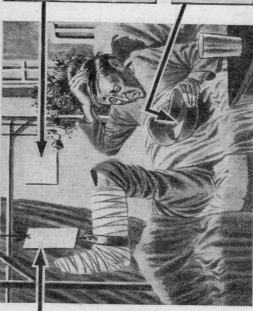

*Each day in this Hospital takes you further into*
**HOPELESS DEBT!**
**HIRE AN AMBULANCE NOW**
AND HAVE THEM DRIVE YOU TO
**THE GREAT NORTHERN FINANCE CO.**
FOR A FRIENDLY HIGH-INTEREST **LOAN**

*DON'T PUT THOSE IMPORTANT FINAL ARRANGEMENTS* IN THE HANDS OF THE **INCOMPETANTS** YOU LEAVE BEHIND!
DO IT YOURSELF **TODAY!**
TOMORROW MAY BE **TOO LATE!**
**Dormant Schlepp & Sons** Licensed Morticians
*"Your last wise move"*

YOU WON'T WANT TO MISS THE THOUGHT-PROVOKING ARTICLE
**"IS YOUR DOCTOR USING YOU FOR A GUINEA PIG?"**
in the current issue of
The Readers' Digest

U.S. INTERNAL REVENUE SERVICE

The World
Looks Brighter When
You Drink...
**OLD OVERSHOE**
100 PROOF ** CONVENIENT HALF-GALLONS
FOR DROWNING MAJOR TROUBLES

SOLVE YOUR
TAX PROBLEMS
THE MODERN WAY!
FLY
to
**PARAGUAY
NOW!**
No Questions Asked.
**Andy's Andes Airlines**

BACK TAXES
Got You
UPSET?
END IT ALL WITH A
**Wise & Heimer
.38 REVOLVER**

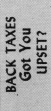

GOLD MEDAL AWARD—
INTERNATIONAL
RUSSIAN
ROULETTE
FESTIVAL

ENDORSED
BY
LEADING
SUICIDES
EVERYWHERE

END —